F. A. Paley, E. S. Crooke

The Ion of Euripides

A new and accurate Translation from the Text of F.A. Paley

F. A. Paley, E. S. Crooke

The Ion of Euripides
A new and accurate Translation from the Text of F.A. Paley

ISBN/EAN: 9783337185961

Printed in Europe, USA, Canada, Australia, Japan

Cover: Foto ©ninafisch / pixelio.de

More available books at **www.hansebooks.com**

THE ION OF EURIPIDES,

A NEW AND ACCURATE

TRANSLATION

FROM THE TEXT OF F. A. PALEY,

With Notes Critical and Explanatory.

BY E. S. CROOKE, B. A.,

Late of Pemb. Coll. Cambridge.

CAMBRIDGE :—J. HALL AND SON;

LONDON :—WHITTAKER & CO; SIMPKIN, MARSHALL & CO.

AND BELL AND DAIDY.

1866.

THE ION, if one of the most beautiful, is in some respects one of the most difficult of Euripides' plays, and the more so, because there are no scholia upon it extant. The edition of Hermann, published forty or fifty years ago, is a valuable one. But the recent edition of Mr. Paley, embodying as it does the corrections and explanations of all the best critics, with his own judicious and valuable remarks, seems far the best that has appeared. The following translation is based upon his text, and I have pretty generally adopted the English versions of particular passages given in his notes: here and there I have ventured to differ from him, but always with reluctance and hesitation. The only thing (and that a minor matter) with which I should be disposed to find any fault, is a peculiarity of punctuation in several places, in which he has, it is clear, too implicitly followed Hermann and other German editors. I have endeavoured to be very literal, perhaps to a fault, and at the same time as far as possible to preserve the spirit of the original Greek. In how many cases I have failed, I am well aware. Any one who has made the attempt, knows the extreme difficulty of combining the *literal* with the *virtual* in the translation of a Greek play.

E. S. C.

June, 1866.

PLOT.

CREUSA, daughter of Erechtheus, having been ravished by Apollo, gave birth to a son, whom she exposed in the grotto which had been the scene of this amour. At the request of Apollo, Mercury brought the infant to his temple at Delphi, and laid him down on the steps. There he was found by the Pythia, and was brought up in the temple, where he was afterwards taken into the special service of the god. In the meanwhile Creusa has married Xuthus. Having no family, but desiring one, they come to Delphi to consult the oracle on the subject, Creusa secretly hoping at the same time to have an opportunity of learning the fate of her offspring. In answer to Xuthus, Apollo bids him salute as his son the first person he should meet on leaving the temple. He meets the son of of Apollo and Creusa, and declares himself his father, naming him Ion, but, to avoid offence to Creusa, bids him keep the matter a secret for the present. Creusa however gets information of it, and attemps to poison Ion. This plot is discovered, and Ion is only prevented from killing her by her taking refuge at Apollo's altar. The Pythia endeavours to calm him, and bids him seek out his mother, taking with him as tokens the cradle or basket in which she found him, and the clothes and ornaments which she has carefully preserved with it. Creusa suddenly recognizes these, and a dénouement takes place.

DRAMATIS PERSONÆ.

————

MERCURY.

ION.

CHORUS OF CREUSA'S HANDMAIDS.

CREUSA.

XUTHUS.

PEDAGOGUE.

MALE ATTENDANT OF CREUSA.

THE PYTHIA.

MINERVA.

SCENE.—DELPHI.

THE ION OF EURIPIDES.

MERCURY. Atlas, who with brazen shoulders upholds heaven the ancient abode of the gods, by one of the goddesses begot Maia, who bore me, Mercury, minister of the deities, to all-great[1] Jove. And I am 5 come to this land of Delphi, where Phœbus occupying the central navel *of the earth* chants *responses* to mortals, ever divining *of* the things that are and are to be.[2] For there is a not obscure city of the Greeks, called *the city* of Pallas of the golden 10 spear, where Phœbus by force subjected to his embraces[3] Creusa daughter of Erechtheus, at that spot in the land of the Athenians where are the northern rocks below the hill of Pallas which the kings of the Attic territory call the Macræ.[4] And unknown to her father (for *so* it was well-pleasing to the god) she bore the burden of her womb; and when the 15 time came, having brought forth a boy in the palace, Creusa bore away the babe to the same cavern

---

1. Lit.—*Greatest.*
2. *i. e. Giving oracular explanations or directions about things that are, and prophesying things that are to be.*
3. Lit.—*Yoked to nuptials.*
4. Lit.—*Where of the land of the Athenians &c. the kings of the Attic territory call the northern rocks the Macræ.*

A

where she had lain[1] with the god, and exposes him
to die[2] in the well-rounded circle of a hollow basket,
20 observing the custom of her forefathers and earth-
born Erichthonius: for to him the daughter of
Jove attached two guardian snakes as protectors
of his person, when she gave him to the Agraulian
25 maids to take care of. Hence there is there a
custom among the Erechthidæ[3] to rear their children
in snakes of beaten gold. Well:[4] having put what
fine raiment the maid had upon the child, about to
die, as she supposed,[5] she left him. And Phœbus,
30 being my brother, makes this request[6] of me; My
brother, go to the earth-born people of renowned
Athens (for thou knowest the city of the goddess),
take the new-born babe and bring him out of the
hollow rock, with the basket itself and the swaddling-
clothes which he has, to my oracle of Delphi, and
35 lay him at the very entrance of my house. And
the rest, for (that thou mayst know it) the boy is
mine, shall be my care.[7] And I, wishing to do[8] a
favour to my brother Loxias, took up the wicker
basket and brought it, and place the boy on the steps
of the temple here, having opened the woven basket of

---

1. Lit—*Lay.*
2. Lit.—*As to die.*
3. Lit.—*For to him the daughter of Jove having attached two
guardian snakes protectors of his person, gives him to &c. whence
there is there a certain custom to the Erechthidæ.* For the
Mythological allusions see Dictionary of Mythology.
     What the poet's exact meaning is in this passage, is not quite
transparent. It seems however to be, that the memory of
Erichthonius' guardian snakes was preserved, in the case of Creusa,
by the round, coil-like shape of the cradle and by the coil or collar
of snakes round the child's neck, and in the case of his later
descendants, by a similar coil or collar which children used to wear.
4. Lit.—*But.*
5. Lit.—*As about to die.*
6. Lit.—*Requests these things.*
7. Lit.—*Shall be a care to us.*
8. Lit.—*Doing.*

the cradle, that the boy might be seen. And early as 40
the orb[1] of the sun riding *forth* the prophetess chances
to enter the oracle of the god, and having cast
her eyes on the infant boy, wondered that[2] any damsel
of the Delphian maids should dare to place her 45
stealthy offspring[3] at the house of the god, and she
was minded to eject him beyond the area *of the temple :*
but for pity she left her cruelty, and the god was
an ally to the boy, that he should not be cast out from
the edifice. And she takes him and rears him : but
she knows not *of* Phœbus who begat him, nor *of* 50
the mother of whom he was born, and the boy is
ignorant of those who gave him birth. He roved
therefore, as long as he was young, sporting about the
altars amid which he was reared :[4] but when his form
grew to manhood, the Delphians made him treasure-
keeper of the god and trusty guardian of all, and 55
in the palace of the god he lives on a holy life to this
very day.[5] And Creusa who bore the youth marries
Xuthus by such coincidence as this : between Athens
and the sons of Chalcodon, who possess the Eubœan 60
land, intervened the flood of war,[6] which having toiled
through with *the Athenians* and aided them with
his spear in driving back,[7] he received the honour
of marriage with Creusa, not being a native *of the
land,* but born an Achæan[8] of Æolus the son of
Jupiter : and having entered into late wedlock, he
is childless, and Creusa : and for this reason they 65

1. Lit.—*Along with the orb.*
2. Lit.—*If.*
3. Lit.—*Labour.*
4. Lit.—*Altar rearings.*
5. Lit.—*Constantly thus far.*
6. Lit.—*There was to Athens &c. a flood of war.*
7. Lit.—*Having jointly taken away.*
8. i. e. *Phthian.*

are come to the oracle here of Apollo through
desire of children. But Loxias puts off his[1] *good* fortunes to this *time*, and he has not been forgotten by
him, as he seems *to be*. For he will present to Xuthus,

70 when he has entered this oracle, his own son, and will
declare that he is his offspring,[2] in order that having
come to his mother's abode, he may be made known
to Creusa, and both the loves of Loxias may be[3] concealed, and the boy may have his rights.[4] And
he will bring it to pass that he be called throughout

75 Greece Ion by name, founder of colonies in the Asiatic
land. But I will go into the laurel coverts here,
that I may learn what is determined about the youth.
For I see the son of Loxias coming out,[5] that he may
make the portico in front of the temple clean with

80 branches of laurel. And I *am the* first of the gods *to*
call him by the name which he is about to obtain, Ion.

Ion. Already the sun is wheeling this *his* bright
chariot of four steeds over the earth, and the stars are

85 flying from the sky *before* these *his* fires into sacred
night, and the untrodden Parnassian peaks illumined
welcome the car[6] of day for mortals. And the smoke

90 of myrrh from desert lands[7] wings its way to the roof
of Phœbus, and the Delphic priestess[8] is sitting on the
divine tripod, chanting to the Greeks the utterances
which Apollo pronounces. But, O ye Delphian mi-

95 nisters of Phœbus, go to the Castalian silvery

---

1. i. e.—*Ion's.*
2. Lit.—*Has been begotten of him* i. e. *Xuthus.*
3. Lit.—*Become.*
4. Lit.—*The things meet.*
5. Lit.—The τόνδε, which is not wanted in the English, denotes
his entrance on the stage.
6. Lit.—*Wheel.*
7. Lit.—*Waterless myrrh.*
8. Lit.—*Woman.* But γυνή is virtually a much higher word.

eddies, and having laved yourselves in the pure dews,
come to the temple: guard a mouth of good omen
and favourable, and utter[1] from your own tongue words
favourable to those who desire to consult the god. 100
And I (a labour which I have ever from a boy
performed) will make the portals of Phœbus bright
with branches of laurel and holy garlands, and the 105
ground moist with sprinkled water,[2] and will put
to flight with my bow and arrows[3] the flocks of
birds which mar the holy offerings; for as
being motherless and fatherless I serve the temple 110
of Phœbus which reared me. Come, O thou new-
grown implement[4] of fairest laurel, which sweepest the
pavement of Phœbus beneath his temple, from im- 115
mortal groves where sacred dews sending forth
their ever-flowing stream lave the sacred foliage of 120
the myrtle, with which the livelong day I sweep
the floor of the god, serving him day by day early
as[5] the fleet wing of the sun. O Pæan, O Pæan,
be thou blessed, blessed, O son of Latona. Honour- 125
able *is* the work *in which* I serve thee, O Phœbus,
before thine house, revering thy oracular abode: 130
and glorious to me is the work to have hands[6] minis-
tering to the gods, *and* not to mortals, but immortals:
and I faint not to labour in works of praise. Phœbus 135
is to me a sire, a father: for I bless him that
nourishes me. And for his benefits to me I call
Phœbus who dwells in the temple by the name of

---

1. Inf. in the imperative sense. The previous clause seems
to imply a negative, as this a positive εὐφημία.
2. Lit.—*Watery sprinklings.*
3. The pl. has very commonly a wider or looser sense than
the singular, as here.
4. Lit.—*O thou service.*—Abstr. for concrete.
5. Lit.—*Together with.*
6. Lit.—*A hand.*

140 father.[1] O Pæan, O Pæan, be thou blessed, blessed, O
son of Latona. But I will cease[2] *from* my labours
145 with the trailing of the laurel, and from golden vessels
will sprinkle on the ground the stream which the
150 eddies of Castalia pour forth, throwing *on it* moisten-
ing water, *all holily, as* being pure from the love
of women. O that I may not cease thus to serve
Phœbus ever, or may cease with happy destiny. Ha !
155 ha ! the winged ones are already on the move and are
leaving their nests on Parnassus:[4] I bid them not
approach the eaves nor to the gold-decked temple.
Once more[5] I will hit thee with my bow and arrows, O
160 thou messenger of Jove, surpassing the strength of *all
other* birds with thy beak. Here is a swan too steer-
ing his flight towards the steps of the temple.[6] Wilt
thou not move thy bright red foot another way? In no
165 way shall the lyre of Phœbus in unison *with thy song*
save thee[7] from my bow : turn aside thy wings : go to
the Delian lake. Thou shalt quench in blood thy
170 sweet-voiced songs, if thou wilt not obey. Ha ! ha !
What fresh bird *is* this *that* has come ? *Is it* to place

---

1. This is somewhat involved, but the literal sense appears
to be—*And according to the beneficial to me I call (the name) of
Phœbus in the temple the name of father.*

2. Lit.—*But (I will now perform another duty,) for I will
cease &c.*

3. The genitive in such a sense is extremely unusual. Commonly
there is the same ethical difference between ῥίπτειν with genitive,
and ῥίπτειν πρός as between *cast at* and *cast on.*

4. Lit.—*The couches of Parnassus.*

5. Either this alludes to Ion's having hit the Eagle on some
former occasion, or it may be taken (preferably perhaps) as elliptical
—*I warn thee once more.*

6. Lit.—*This here another swan is rowing towards the area*—ἄλλος
used in the same way as it is in οἱ ἄνδρες καὶ αἱ ἄλλαι γυναῖκες,
or as the superlative in ἀξιολογώτατος τῶν προγεγενημένων.
Θυμέλη (1) *An altar:* (2) *the quasi-altar of Dionysus in a Greek
theatre, on a rectangular platform ascended by steps:* hence (3)
generally, *a platform, an area:* and hence (4) *the platform or
area, ascended by steps, on which a temple stood:* perhaps (5) *these
steps.*

7. Lit.—*Should save thee (if thou thoughtest so).*

a nest of dry twigs beneath the eaves for its young ones? The twanging of the bow shall prevent thee. Wilt thou not obey? Go and breed in the eddies 175 of Alpheus, or to the Isthmian glen, that the offerings and temple of Phœbus be not interfered with. For I am loth to slay you that announce the oracles of 180 the gods to mortals: but I will serve Phœbus in the work to which I am devoted, and will not cease to minister to those who nourish me.

CHORUS.

Cho. A. Not in divine Athens only were there dwellings of the gods decked with fair columns, nor 185 *there only* the service of Agyieus: but in the house of Loxias also the son of Latona is there the fair-eyed light of the twin countenances.[1]

Cho. B. Lo! see here;[2] the son of Jupiter is 190 slaying the Lernæan hydra with golden scimetar: dear *sister*, behold *this* with thine eyes.

Cho. A. I see. And near him another is raising 195 a blazing torch. Who is this? Is it the warrior Iolaus whose story is related to me as I work at my loom,[3] who undertaking a common labour with the son 200 of Jove is helping him to accomplish it?

Cho. C. And look too at this *hero* mounted on winged steed: he is slaying the fire-breathing three-formed monster.[4]

Cho. A. Yes, I am directing my eyes[5] all 205

---

1. *i. e.* The images of Apollo and Diana, painted on the walls. *Heath.*
2. Lit.—*This here* (sc. *the hydra*).
3. Lit.—*Who is related in story beside my web* i. e. *whose story is related to me by some one at my side, that I may weave a representation of it.*
4. Lit.—*Might.*
5. Lit.—*Eyelid.*

around. Observe the conflict with the giants on the stone walls.

Cho. D. We are looking here, dear *sisters,* * * *

Cho. E. Seest thou then one brandishing her 210 gorgon shield against Enceladus?

Cho. F. I see Pallas my own deity.

Cho. G. Why, *dost thou not see* the mighty thunderbolt all-blazing in the far-darting hands of Jove?

Cho. H. I see: he is burning up the hostile 215 Mimus with the flames.

Cho. I. And Bromius Bacchus is slaying another of the sons of earth with unwarlike ivy-bound staff.

Cho. A. To thee I call who art by the temple,— 220 is it lawful to ascend to the shrine, I mean[1] with pure-washed foot * * *?

Ion. It is not lawful, stranger-maids.

Cho. K. And might I not enquire a word from thee?

Ion. What then wilt thou?

Cho. L. Does the house of Phœbus really occupy the central navel of the earth?

Ion. Ay, clad in garlands, and on either hand are Gorgons.

225   Cho. M. So also rumour declares.

Ion. If you have offered a cake before the temple, and ye desire to enquire aught of Phœbus, pass on to the steps: but without sheep sacrificed[2] pass not into the chambers of the house.

230   Cho. N. I understand: and we offer not to

---

1. The force of γέ, limiting the question. If the passage is to be taken as it stands, I know of no other intelligible way of translating it. But it is evidently imperfect, perhaps quite corrupt.
2. Lit.—*On condition of sheep unsacrificed.*

transgress[1] the law of the god; but that which is
without shall delight our eye.

Ion. Survey all with your eyes, everything which
it is lawful *to behold.*

Cho. o. My lord and lady[2] have allowed me to
come forth to see this shrine.[3]

Ion. And of what house are ye called the
handmaids?

Cho. p. The halls that nurtured my lord and 235
lady are the abode of Pallas. And here she is of
whom thou questionest me[4].

Ion. High birth hast thou, and this mien of thine
indicates thy rank,[5] whoever thou art, O lady. For
any one may tell for the most part about man or 240
woman, when he has observed their mien, if they
are nobly born.[6] But, O, thou hast made me wonder
because thou hast closed thine eyes and bedewed
thy high-born cheek with tears, when thou beheldest
the holy oracle of Loxias. What grief *is* this into
which thou art come, O lady? Where all else rejoice 245
at beholding the shrine of the god, there[7] thine eye
sheds tears.

Creusa. O stranger, thou art not unkind to
marvel at my tears:[8] but when I saw this temple
of Apollo, I retraced certain memories *of the* past, and 250
somehow while I was here had my thoughts at home.

---

1. Force of the present.
2. See note on 108.
3. As before in 220. Lit.—*These recesses.*
4. Lit.—*The roof-trees nutritive of my lords are indwelt of
Pallas, and about this woman here being present thou questionest me.*
5. Lit.—*And thou hast this mien here a proof of thy ways of life.*
6. Lit.—*About a human being......if it is by nature of good birth.*
7. Lit.—*Here.*
8. Lit.—*Thine has itself in a way not lacking (the humanizing
effects of) education to come into wonderments about my tears.*

O hapless women! O daring deeds of the gods!
What then *shall we say?* Whither shall we refer
our claims for justice, if we are to be outraged by the
unjust acts of those that rule *the world?*

255   Ion. But why art thou secretly sad at heart,
lady?

Cr. 'Tis nought, I have shot my bolt:[1] and
henceforth I am silent, and do thou no more think
of this.

Ion. And who art thou? From what part of the
land hast thou come? Of what father art thou sprung?
By what name must I call thee?

260   Cr. My name is Creusa, and I am a daughter of
Erechtheus, and my native land is the city of the
Athenians.

Ion. O inhabiting a renowned city, and bred
of noble ancestors, how I honour thee, lady.

Cr. Thus far I am really[1] fortunate, O stranger,
but no further.

265   Ion. By the gods *I pray thee*, did in truth (as he
is declared by men)—

Cr. What *it is* thou askest, O stranger, I would
know.

Ion. A forefather of thy father spring from
the earth?

Cr. Yes; Erichthonius *did:* but my descent
avails me nought.

Ion. And did Minerva take him up from the
earth?

270   Cr. Yes, though she bore him not, into her
virgin hands.

---

1. i. e. *I have said my say.*
2. Καί, *really,* seems to add a *fact* to the *appearance* of one.

Ion. And she entrusts him, as is commonly represented in the picture—?

Cr. Yes, to the daughters of Cecrops to take care of without being seen *by them.*

Ion. I have heard that the maids opened the chest of the goddess.

Cr. For that reason they died and stained the crag of the rock with their blood.

Ion. Well. What then *of* this? is the story 275 a truth or falsely *told?*

Cr. What *is it* thou askest? for I am not tired of attending to thee.[1],

Ion. Did thy father Erechtheus sacrifice thy sisters?

Cr. He forced himself[2] to slay the maids as sacrifices for the land.

Ion. But how wast thou the only one of thy sisters[3] saved?

Cr. I was a new-born babe in the arms of my 280 mother.

Ion. And does afterwards a yawning of the earth really swallow up thy father?

Cr. A blow from the trident of the sea destroyed him.

Ion. And the place there is called Macræ?

Cr. Why dost thou ask this? How hast thou reminded me of a certain event!

---

1. Σχολάζειν τινι = *vacare alicui, to give heed to a person, bestow one's time on him, do all one can for him.* Here σχολή in a corresponding sense.

2. For the various meanings of τλῆναι see, very good ones in Monk's Alcestis.

3. See note on 162. Though "the only one of thy sisters" will hardly stand in plain prose, Milton has not hesitated to say "the fairest of her daughters, Eve", and therefore I see no objection to retaining the Grecism here.

285   Ion. Pythius honours it *with his presence*, and the bright light of Pythius?

Cr. He does honour it *with his presence*. Honour it indeed[1]! O that I had never seen him *there*.

Ion. But why? Dost thou hate that which the god best loves?

Cr. 'Tis no matter: I know of a deed which is the shame of the caves.[2]

Ion. And what husband of the Athenians married thee, lady?

290   Cr. Not a citizen, but a stranger from another land.

Ion. Who? He must be one of noble birth.

Cr. Xuthus, sprung from Æolus and from Jupiter.

Ion. And how being a foreigner did he wed thee being a native?

Cr. Eubœa is a neighbouring state to Athens:

295   Ion. Bounded, as they say, by watery bounds.

Cr. This he ravaged with spear united to the Cecropidæ.

Ion. Having come as an ally, and then he weds thy couch?

Cr. Yes, receiving me as a dowry of war and reward of his spear.

Ion. And art thou come to the oracle with thy husband or alone?

300   Cr. With my husband. But he is visiting the shrine of Trophonius.

Ion. As a spectator, or for the sake of oracles?

Cr. Wishing to learn one thing both from him and from Phœbus.

---

1. Lit.—*What does he honour it?*
2. Lit.—*I am cognizant with the caves of a certain shame (to them).*

Ion. And are ye come about the fruits of the land, or respecting children?

Cr. We are childless, though we have had a long wedded life.

Ion. And hast thou never yet borne any offspring, 305 but art barren?

Cr. Phœbus knows how true it is that I am childless.[1]

Ion. O unhappy *lady*, how unfortunate thou art, in all else fortunate!

Cr. But who art thou? How blessed in thee have I deemed her who bore thee!

Ion. I am called and am the servant of the god, O lady.

Cr. An offering from the city, or having been 310 sold by some one?

Ion. I know not, save one thing—I am called *the servant* of Loxias.

Cr. I then in turn, O stranger, mutually pity thee.

Ion. As not knowing who bore me and of what father I was begotten.

---

1. In the preceding lines there is evidently an Euripidean refinement of distinction between *ἄπαις* and *ἄτεκνος*—*ἄπαις who has no children at the present time*, *ἄτεκνος* (*ἡ οὐ τεκοῦσα*) *who has never borne children*. We must not, I think, regard the assertion in this 306th line as a direct falsehood, but as an equivocation, which again is one of Euripides' special delights. Creusa evidently intends Ion to understand her words, as a solemn asseveration, that *she* is *childless*, especially as she had already said *ἄπαιδες ἐσμεν* (apparently the same thing, really very different). But her words also had a reserved meaning—*Phœbus knows* (*the degree of*) *my childlessness* i. e. *whether my child yet lives or not*. This way of speaking (in which a word, without any necessarily intended equivocation, may virtually get the meaning of its opposite) is not uncommon in Greek, and the larger Grammars will supply sufficient examples of it. I have endeavoured, as best I could, to preserve the equivoque of the original. All the three lines are thoroughly Euripidean.

CR. And dwellest thou in this temple, or at home?

315   ION. All the abode of the god is mine, wherever sleep may come upon me.

CR. And didst thou come to the temple when thou wast a boy, or a young man?

ION. Those who appear to know say *that I came as* a babe.

CR. And who of the women of Delphi reared thee with her milk?

ION. Never did I know the breast. But she who reared me *was*—

320   CR. Who, O hapless one? How being troubled have I found troubles.

ION. The prophetess of Phœbus; I regard her as a mother.

CR. And possessed of what maintenance, hast thou arrived at manhood?

ION. The altars fed me and the stranger that came from time to time.

CR. To be pitied then was she that bore thee, whoever she was.

325   ION. I was *the fruit* perchance *of* some woman's error.

CR. And thou hast a livelihood? for thou art handsomely decked in robes.

ION. I am arrayed in the garb of the god, whom I serve.

CR. And didst thou not go in search to discover thy parentage?

ION. No, lady, for I have no token of it.

330   CR. Alas! Another woman has suffered the same *troubles* as thy mother.

ION. Who? I should rejoice, if she would sympathize with my misfortunes.

CR. She for whose sake I came hither before my husband should arrive.

ION. What manner of thing desiring? as I will give thee my services, lady.

CR. Wishing to learn a secret oracle from Phœbus.

ION. Speak: I will arrange for thee all the rest. 335

CR. Hear then the story. But I am ashamed—

ION. Thou wilt accomplish nothing then: the goddess (Αἰδώς) is an inactive *deity*.

CR. One of my friends declares that she had intercourse with Phœbus.

ION. A woman born, with Phœbus? Say not so, stranger *lady*.

CR. Yes, and bore a son to the god unknown 340 to her father.

ION. Impossible! She is ashamed of seduction by a man.

CR. She herself says that it is not so: and she has suffered sad *griefs*.

ION. What doing? since she was united with a god.

CR. She *carried forth* the son which she bore out of the house *and* exposed *him*.

ION. And where is the boy which was exposed? 345 does he behold the light?

CR. None knows. This would I learn from the oracle.[1]

ION. But if he is no more, in what manner did he perish?

CR. She supposes that wild beasts killed him, poor *boy*.

---

1. The καί seems to imply—*I am ignorant of this, and also would learn, &c.*

ION. What evidence had she to make her think this ?[1]

350   CR. When she went *to the place* where she had exposed him, she found him no longer there.

ION. And were there any drops of blood in the way ?

CR. She says there were not, although she traversed the ground oft.

ION. And how long is it since the child was destroyed ?[2]

CR. If he were alive, he would have the same measure of youth as thou.

355   ION. Did[3] she not then afterwards bear any other child ?

CR. The god seduced her : but she has borne no other and is wretched.

ION. But what, if Phœbus has taken him and is rearing him up secretly.

CR. He does not right to rejoice alone *in a subject of* common rejoicing.[4]

ION. Alas ! his fortunes are in harmony with my fate.

360   CR. After thee too, O stranger, I ween that a wretched mother yearns.

ION. Yet tempt me not to a grief which I have forgotten.

CR. I am silent. But go on with those matters about which I ask thee.

---

1. Lit.—*What sort of evidence using did she think this ?*
2. Lit.—*And what time is there to the child having been made an end of ?*
3. Lit.—*Does.* The histor. pres. does not quite always bear a literal translation. So ἀδικεῖ below.
4. i. e. *His mother is entitled to rejoice in the boy's safety as well as the god.*

Ion. Knowest thou then what *feature* of thy story involves most difficulty ?

Cr. And what *is there that* does not with her, poor *soul*, go wrong ?

Ion. How shall the god declare what he wishes to 365 be concealed ?

Cr. *He will*, since he is seated on the common tripod of Greece.

Ion. He is ashamed of his deed. Seek not to convict him.[1]

Cr. But still she who suffered from it is distressed by her misfortunes.

Ion. There is not any who will reveal these things to thee. For Phœbus being made to appear 370 guilty in his own temple would with reason work some ill to him that delivered the oracle to thee : Cease, lady : we must not by oracles enquire into what is adverse to the god. For to such *a height* of folly should we come, if we shall constrain the gods against 375 their will to declare the things that they would not, either by the sacrifices of sheep before their altars, or through auguries by birds. For the good things which[2] we seek after against the will of the gods *and* in spite *of them*, we gain nothing by possessing,[3] O 380 lady : but by those which they grant willingly, we are benefited.

Cho. Many are the misfortunes of many amongst mortals, and the forms of them differ. But scarcely can one ever find one *unvarying course of* prosperity in the life of men.

---

1. See note on 231.
2. Ἄν = ἅ ἄν.
3. Lit.—*We possess not being.*

Cr. O Phœbus, both in that and in this thou art
385 unjust to her who is absent from thee,[1] *but* whose request is present. Neither hast thou protected thy
son, whom thou shouldest have protected, nor being a
prophet wilt thou inform his mother when she en-
quires of thee, in order that, if he is no more, he may
be honoured with a tomb, but, if he is *alive*, he
390 may come to behold his mother[2] at last. But I must
investigate this matter *by myself*, if, I am forbidden[3]
by the god to learn what I wish. But, O stranger,
(for I see my noble spouse Xuthus already near,
having quitted the caves of Trophonius) say nought to
395 my husband of the words which have been spoken, lest
I should incur any reproach by undertaking secret
missions, and the story may be spread[4] not quite
in the way in which I was unfolding it to thee. For
the position of women is difficult with respect to men,
400 and we are liable to be hated[5] *all alike*, the good con-
founded with the bad: so unfortunate are we.

Xuthus. First, *all* hail the god, receiving the
prime offerings of my salutations, and thou *next*,
my lady. Have I alarmed thee with fears by the
lateness of my coming?[6]

Cr. In no wise, but thou hast come as I was beginning to be anxious.[7] However tell me what

---

1. There seems to be a *double entente* in τὴν ἀποῦσαν.
2. Lit.—*Into the sight of his mother*, which may either mean
to see his mother, or *to be seen by his mother.*
3. Κωλύω is *to prevent*: the sense of *forbid* is due to the tense.
See note on 231.
4. Lit.—*Advance.*
5. The present here is, strictly speaking, *habitual* in sense.
6. Lit.—*Having come after a long time.*
7. Lit.—*Thou camest in time for my anxiety (to be stopped)*.
Paley explains the passage differently, perhaps better. But the
interpretation here given avoids an unnaturalness (if his explanation
be adopted) in the subsequent dialogue, arising from the omission of
all enquiry on the part of Xuthus into the cause of his wife's grief.

response thou bringest from Trophonius, how a seed of 405
children shall be obtained by us.

Xu. He thought it not right to anticipate the response of the god: but one thing he said, that
I should not go home from the oracle, nor thou,
childless.

Cr. O revered mother of Phœbus, may *it be* with 410
good omen *that* we have come *hither*, and may our
former votive offerings to thy son change and become
more auspicious[1].

Xu. This will be. But who is interpreter for the
god?

Ion. I am without, but things within are
entrusted to others, who sit near the tripod, O 415
stranger, nobles of the Delphians, to whom the lot has
fallen.

Xu. 'Tis well: I have learned now all that
I wanted. I will go in: for, as I hear, the common
victim for the visitors to the oracle has fallen in front
of the temple: and I desire this day, for it is a pro- 420
pitious one, to receive the response of the god. And

---

3. Lit.—*May the votive offerings to thy son which were to us
before, by a change fall out better.*
    In this remarkably difficult passage, Paley follows Hermann, who
says—*Quod nobis prius cum filio tuo commercii intercessit melius
cadat.* Ita Xutho videbitur orare, ut quæ nunc sacra facturi sint,
magis propitia menteacci piat Apollo, quam quæ ei antehac fuerint
oblata: ipsa autem orat, ut quæ sibi olim infelix fuit cum Apolline
consuetudo, quippe cujus præmium orbitatem habet, ea ut in melius
convertatur, ereptumque sibi filium inveniat.—I can understand the
first explanation, but the second I cannot. For νῷν undoubtedly =
nobis, and *nobis* as undoubtedly = *mihi*: but is it true that νῷν =
mihi? If not, are we to take νῷν to mean *Apollo and me?* Then what
is the meaning of ἐς παῖδα τὸν σόν, *Apollo* again? It makes nonsense.
The "double entente" must, I fear, be given up, though the passage
at first sight, presents every appearance of one. Though I can see
nothing in the commentators better than Hermann's first explanation,
it is not one which very naturally belongs to the words, and
I am inclined to believe that the passage has not yet been
properly understood.

do thou, my lady, take branches of laurel and at[1] the altars pray to the gods that I may bring away from the house of Apollo a response granting children to us.

425   CR. This shall be *done*, it shall be. But if Loxias should choose even now[2] to make amends for his former misdeeds, he would not be all favourable to us, but whatever he deigns, for he is a god, will I accept.

     ION. What can be the reason why[3] the stranger-
430 lady is constantly speaking by dark hints *and* throwing out reproaches against the god in secret speeches? *Is it* either because she loves her on whose behalf she consults the god, or else[4] because she would conceal something which need be concealed?[5] But what care I for the daughter of Erectheus? She is nought to me.[6] Well, I will go and with golden
435 pitchers place water in the lavers. But I must remind Phœbus what he is doing: he deflowers virgins by force and deserts them: he begets children clandestinely and suffers them to die. *Do* not thou *thus:* but, since thou art mighty, pursue virtuous
440 deeds. For whoever among mortals is evil, him the gods chastise. How then is it right that ye, having laid down the law for mortals, should yourselves be guilty of breaking the law? But if ye (it will not be so, but I will use the argument) shall make satis-
445 faction to men for your forcible amours, thou and

---

1. Lit.—*About.*
2. Νῦν ἀλλά i. e. εἰ μὴ πρότερον, ἀλλὰ νῦν.
3. Lit.—*Why ever?*
4. Lit.—*Or also.*
5. Lit.—*Something of the things which it is necessary should be kept silent.*
6. Lit.—*She nought appertains to me.*

Neptune and Jove who rules the sky, you will empty[1]
your temples to pay the penalties of your wrong deeds.
For ye do wrong by your eagerness for your pleasures
in preference to reason: no more is it right to
call men evil, since we imitate the evil deeds of 450
the gods, but those who teach them these things.

CHO. I beseech thee, my *patron goddess* Minerva,
who didst need no Ilithyia to assist at the pangs
of thy birth,[2] brought forth from the crown of Jove's 455
head by Promethean Titan, O thou august Vic-
tory, fly from the golden chambers of Olympus
to the public ways and come to the Pythian 460
abode, where the Phœbean shrine in the mid-
navel of the earth delivers unfailing[3] oracles at
the choir-girt tripod, thou and the maid Latona-born, 465
two goddesses, two virgins, revered sisters of Phœbus.
And supplicate him, O maidens, that the ancient
race of Erectheus may obtain the blessing of off- 470
spring, though late, by his holy responses. For
it[4] involves[5] surpassing happiness, an undisturbed fund
of joy, to mortals to whom youthful scions of children 475
flourish[6] fruitful in their fathers' halls, to keep[7] wealth
inherited from their fathers for other children: for 480
it is an aid in troubles, and with good fortune it
is a delightful thing, and it brings protecting aid
to their native land with the spear. To me before 485
wealth and royal nuptials be a dear offspring of
beloved children. But I abhor childless life, and

---

1. i. e. *Of treasure.*
2. Lit.—*Ilithyia-less of birth-pangs.*
3. Lit.—*Accomplishes.*
4. Sc. εὐτεκνία.
5. Lit.—*Has (in it).*
6. Lit.—*Shine.*
7. "Εξοντες—Constr. κατὰ σύνεσιν, agrees with παῖδες implied in
ἥβαι.

I blame him for whom it has charms:[1] and, with
490 moderate possessions in life, may I be reckoned blest
with children. O ye abodes of Pan and thou rock
neighbouring to the cavernous Macræ, where the three
495 daughters of Agraulos[2] foot it in the dance o'er the
green course[3] before the temple of Pallas, to the varied
500 sound of the strains *of thy pipe*, when thou pipest,
O Pan, in thy rustic cave, where a maid, O wretched
one! having brought forth a babe to Phœbus, exposed
it as a banquet to birds and a bloody repast to
505 wild beasts, the offspring of forced embraces bearing
bitter fruit.[4] Neither in *works of* the loom *have
I seen it*, nor in story have I heard[5] the fame that
children of mortals by the gods partake of a happy
destiny.

510 ION. Ye attendant women, who wait for your
master, keeping watch about the steps of this incensed
temple, has Xuthus already quitted the sacred
tripod and oracle, or is he staying *yet* in the house enquiring of his childless condition?

CHO. He is in the temple, O stranger: he comes
not forth from this house as yet. But I hear the
515 noise of the doors here, as if he were at the portals, and now thou mayst see my lord coming out.

---

1. Lit.—*To whom it seems good.*
2. Viz. *Agraulos, Herse* and *Pandrosus*, daughters of *Cecrops
and Agraulos.*
3. The construction appears to be Χορους στείβουσι ποδοῖν στάδια,
taking στάδια as the object of the compound expression χορους
στείβουσι ποδοῖν. See the larger grammars for other examples of this
peculiar Grecism.
4. Lit.—*The violence of bitter nuptials*, where the *cause* is put
for the *effect.*
5. Ἄϊον used by Zeugma with ἐπὶ κερκίσιν as well as λόγοις
φάτιν. So Æsch. Prom. Vinct. (in init.) "Ιν' οὔτε φωνὴν οὔτε του
μορφὴν βροτῶν "Οψει.

Xu. All well to thee, my child (for it becomes me to address thee first[1]).

Ion. All's well with me: but be thou in thy sober senses, and two of us will be the better for it.[2]

Xu. Give me to kiss thy hand and to embrace thy body.

Ion. Art thou in thy sober senses, O stranger, or 520 has some curse of the god driven thee mad?

Xu. I am in my senses, since, having found my best beloved, I seek to embrace him.

Ion. Hold, touch not the fillets of the god nor break them with thy hand.

Xu. I will touch thee and *yet* I seek not to tear thee away,[3] but I have found[4] my beloved *child*.

Ion. Wilt thou not let me go, before thou receivest my arrows in thy lungs?

Xu. Why, I pray, wouldst thou fly[5] from me, now 525 that thou hast discovered thy own dearest *parent?*

Ion. I love not to bring rude and crazy strangers to their senses.

Xu. Slay me, burn me: well, if thou slay me, thou wilt be the murderer of thy father.

Ion. And how art thou my father? Is not this laughable for me to hear?

Xu. No: My account *of the matter* will quickly shew thee who I am.[6]

Ion. And what *is it* thou wilt tell me?   530

---

1. Lit.—*For the beginning of speaking is becoming to me.*
2. Lit.—*And we, being two, shall fare well.* Paley explains this differently. But I believe the above version is right. We must suppose Xuthus, as he said ὦ τέκνον, χαῖρε, to have added some demonstrative expression of his paternal love, such as seeking to embrace him. Ion naturally repels this familiarity.
3. 'Ρυσιάζω—lit.—*to seize a pledge as a matter of right.* See also note on 231.
4. Lit.—*I find.*
5. See note on 231.
6. Lit.—*Running would shew thee my affairs.*

Xʊ. I am thy father, and thou art my son.

Ioɴ. Who declares so?

Xʊ. Loxias who reared thee, being *really* mine.

Ioɴ. Thou to thyself art witness.

Xʊ. Yes, but after learning the oracle of the god.

Ioɴ. Thou didst mistake, having heard some ambiguous response.

Xʊ. Then my ears deceive me.[1]

Ioɴ. What now are Phœbus' words?

Xʊ. That he who met me—

535   Ioɴ. Met thee how?[2]

Xʊ. As I came out from this temple of the god—

Ioɴ. What then of him?[3]

Xʊ. Was my son.

Ioɴ. Thine born, or the gift *to thee* of others?

Xʊ. A gift, but of me begotten.

Ioɴ. And thy footsteps first fall in with me?[4]

Xʊ. None else, my child.

Ioɴ. Whence can the strange event have come to pass?[5]

Xʊ. We twain marvel at one *strange event alike.*

540   Ioɴ. Good heavens! But of what mother was I born to thee?

Xʊ. I cannot tell.

Ioɴ. And did not Phœbus say?

Xʊ. At this rejoiced, I questioned not of that.

Ioɴ. I sprung, it seems then, from the earth as my mother.

Xʊ. The ground brings not forth children.

Ioɴ. How then should I be thine?

---

1. Lit.—*Then I hear not aright.*
2. Lit.—(*Met thee*) *what meeting?* cogn. acc.
3. Lit.—*Fell in with what event?*
4. Lit.—*Thou joinest thy foot first indeed with me.*
5. Lit.—*Whence ever has the fortune come (to us)?*

Xu. I know not, but I refer *the confirmation of it* to the god.

Ion. Come, let us take up other discourse.

Xu. '*Twere* better *to do* this, my son.

Ion. Didst thou *ever* approach any illegitimate 545 bed ?

Xu. In the folly of youth.

Ion. Before thou tookest *to wife* the daughter of Erectheus ?

Xu. Yes; for never yet have I since *approached* *any.*

Ion. Didst thou then beget me thus ?[1]

Xu. There is a correspondence in time at least.

Ion. And then how could I come[2] hither ?

Xu. I am at a loss *to tell* this.

Ion. And accomplish so long a journey ?[3]

Xu. This confounds me too.

Ion. And camest thou *ever* before to the Pythian 550 rock ?

Xu. Yes, to the orgies[4] of Bacchus.

Ion. And didst thou tarry in *the house* of any of the public hosts ?

Xu. *One,* who with the Delphian maids—

Ion. Joined thee in the Bacchic dances ? or what meanest thou ?[5]

Xu. Yes with the Mænades of Bacchus.

Ion. Whilst thou was in thy senses, or drunk with wine ?

---

1. Lit.—*There.*
2. Porson on Eurip. Phœn. 1373 lays it down that πῶς καὶ, ποῦ καὶ &c. simply ask for information, but καὶ πῶς, καὶ ποῦ &c. mark an objection or contradiction. This will be most clearly expressed in the present passage by inserting *could.*
3. Lit.—*Having come through the long way.*
4. Lit.—*Torches* or *torch-processions.*
5. Lit.—*How* (i. e. *in what sense*) *sayest thou these things?*

Xu. In the pleasures of Bacchus.

Ion. This is the source whence I was sprung.[1]

Xu. Fate hath found thee, my child.

555 Ion. And how came I to the temple?

Xu. A cast-away perhaps *by the hands* of the maiden.

Ion. I have escaped the *fate of* servile *origin.*

Xu. Receive thy father then, my child.

Ion. It is not meet indeed to disbelieve the god,

Pu. Then thou art wise.

Ion. And what else *should* I wish—

Xu. Now thou seest as thou shouldest see.

Ion. Than to be born son of the son of Jove?

Xu. Which falls to thy lot.

560 Ion. Shall I indeed embrace him that begot me?

Xu. Yes, in obedience to the god.

Ion. Hail, father.

Xu. Joyous those accents have I heard.

Ion. And *hail,* thou day now present.

Xu. Yes, happy has it made me.

Ion. O mother dear, shall I ever[2] see thy form also? Now long I more than ever[3] to behold thee, 565 whoever thou art. But perhaps thou art dead, and I can never[4] *behold thee.*

Cho. Shared by us are the good fortunes of thy house: but still I had wished that our mistress also and the race of Erectheus were happy in possessing children.[5]

---

1. Lit.—*This is that where we were begotten.*
2. Πότ' ἀρά i. e. ἀρά τοτε, *unquamne?* Vide præfat. ad Soph. Œdip. Col. p. 18. Hermann. But see Paley's note.
3. Lit.—*Before.*
4. Lit.—*Nought, in no way.*
5. Lit.—*As to children.*

Xu. My son, as to thy recovery the god has duly
accomplished *the oracle*, and he hath both united thee 570
to me, and thou on thy part hast discovered thy dear
parent, not knowing him before. But what thou hast
rightly with *so much* eagerness desired, this I too long
for[1] that thou, my son, mayst discover thy mother,
and her, I of whom thou wast brought forth. And, if we
leave it to time, we may perhaps discover this. But 575
quit the temple of the god and thy unsettled life,[2] and
yielding thy will to thy father come to Athens, where
the prosperous sceptre of thy father awaits thee and
abundant wealth; and thou wilt not, though unfortunate in one respect,[3] be called at the same time 580
ignobly born and poor, but high-born and rich in
substance. Art thou silent? Why keepest thou thine
eye fixed on the ground?[4] And thou art lost in
thought,[5] and changed again from thy joyfulness
inspirest fears in thy father.[6]

Ion. The face of things whilst they are at a 585
distance, and when looked at close, appears not the
same. I embrace my fortune in having discovered
thee as my father: but hear about what I am thinking
on. They say that the famed earth-born Athens is no 590
alien race, and there[7] I shall fall under two disadvan-
tages which I possess,[8] being of an alien father and
myself of bastard birth. And having this reproach, I

---

1. Lit.—*This a longing possesses me too.*
2. Lit.—*The floor of the god and thy wanderings.*
3. Lit.—*In one thing of two* i. e. *in not knowing thy mother.*
4. Lit.—*Why having cast thine eye to the ground keepest thou it
(there)?*
5. Lit.—*Thou art gone away into thoughts.*
6. Lit.—*Addest fear to thy father.*
7. Lit.—*Where.*
8. Lit.—*Shall fall into two disabilities, possessing them.*

shall be esteemed * * * nought and of mean birth,[1] if
595 destitute of power: but if aiming at the first seat in
the vessel[2] of the state, I seek to be something, I shall
be hated by the humbler sort:[3] for superiors are
obnoxious to them: and amongst all that, being
good and enduring to be wise, hold their peace and
600 are not eager to engage in *state* affairs, I shall incur
ridicule and the charge of folly[4], because I keep not quiet
in a city full of censure: and I shall be the more
jealously guarded by the votes of those on the other
hand who are eloquent and follow politics, if I attain to
605 eminence. For thus, my father, are these things wont
to be: those who possess political power and eminence,
are most hostile to their rivals. And when I come an
intruder to a strange house, and to a childless lady,
who, sharing thy misfortune with thee before, *but* now
610 having ceased to be of equal lot,[5] will bear her fate
alone with bitter sorrowing, how[6] shall I fail to be
naturally hated by her, when I stand by thee near thy
foot, and she, childless as she is, beholds thy beloved
one with bitter jealousy, and then either thou
abandonest me and hast regard to thy wife, or
615 upholdest me, and embroilest thy house? How many
ways of blood-shed and destruction by deadly poisons
have women invented for men. And moreover I pity
thy wife, my father, growing old *still* childless: for,
620 born of noble ancestors, she ought not to lack children
to continue the race. Of royalty that is falsely praised,

---

1. Lit.—*Of no (parents).*
2. Lit.—*Rower's bench.*
3. Lit.—*The powerless.*
4. Lit.—*Folly*—cause for effect. Comp. Eurip. Med. 298. Χωρὶς
γὰρ ἄλλης ἧς ἔχουσιν ἀργίας Φθόνον πρὸς ἀστῶν ἀλφάνουσι δυσμενῆ.
5. Lit.—*Now having obtained a lot apart (from thee).*
6. Δέ is merely the former δέ (ἐλθὼν δέ......) repeated in the
apodosis.

the outside indeed is pleasing, but the domestic state
is grievous: for who is happy, who is fortunate, that
spends[1] his life in fear and in apprehension of violence?[2] And I would choose to live having the good for- 625
tune to be a commoner rather than a monarch, to whom
it is a pleasure to have bad men for his friends, but
he hates good men, fearing to be put to death.   Thou
wilt say that gold outweighs this, and that it is
pleasing to the rich: I love not to hear reproaches 630
because I keep my wealth in my hands, or to incur
trouble.   Be mine the mean, and no disturbing cares.[3]
Now hear from me, my father, what blessings I had
here: first, leisure which is very dear to men, and
little disturbance: nor did any ruffian *ever* drive 635
me from the path; for this[4] is unendurable—to yield
to the baser *sort* and make way for them.   And I was[5]
engaged in prayers to the gods or converse with men,
attending on those well pleased *and* not murmuring.
And to some visitors I would[6] bid farewell, and others 640
would come, so that I was always cheerful being new
to new *comers*.   And (what should be prayed for by
men, even though it should be against their will[7]) duty
and natural disposition led me to be faithful to the
god.   Considering *all* these things, I deem my life 645
here better than living there, O my father.   Permit
me to live in my own way:[8] for equal is the delight to

---

    1. Τείνει may perhaps mean something more than this—*drags
out.*
    2. Lit.—*Casting a sheep's eye on violence.*
    3. Lit.—*But to me be moderate things, not being grieved.*
    4. Lit.—*That.*
    5. Ἦ—a rare form of ἦν. Hermann reads ἦν, which seems
preferable in tragic dialogue.
    6. Force of the imperfect—habit.
    7. Lit.—*To them unwilling.*
    8. Lit.—*For myself.*

rejoice in great possessions, or[1] to have a little and be pleased.

CHO. Well hast thou said, if those whom I love, shall find happiness in thy words.

650   XU. Cease from this discourse, and learn to be happy : for I wish to make a beginning,[2] my son, at the very place where I have found you, by joining in[3] the common feast of a common table, and to offer the sacrifices which I offered not before in acknowledgement of thy birth.[4] And for the present, I will take thee as 655 merely[5] a guest at my hearth and entertain thee with banquets; and I will take thee as a supposed[6] visitor come to see the land of the Athenians, as if thou wert not my son. For I wish not to pain my wife, childless as she is, by my own happiness. But in time, taking 660 a proper occasion, I will induce my spouse to let thee hold my sceptre over the land. And I name thee Ion,[7] a name suited to thy destinies, because thou wast the first to present thy footstep to me as I came out from the shrine of the god. But gather together the crew of thy friends, and with feast of slaughtered ox[8] bid 665 them *farewell*, before thou quittest[9] the Delphian city. And I bid you, ye handmaids, say nought of these matters, or, if ye tell them to my spouse, I threaten you with death.[10]

---

1. Lit.—*And.*
2. Sc. τῆς σῆς εὐτυχίας implied in εὐτυχεῖν.
3. In πεσών there is an allusion perhaps to the reclining attitude of banqueters. *Paley.*
4. Lit.—*Natal of thee.*
5. This seems to be the force of δή.
6. Δῆθεν
7. From ἰών. *going.*
8. Lit.—*With ox-slaughtered enjoyment.*
9. Lit.—*Being about to quit.*
10. Lit.—I (*declare*) *death to you having told &c.*

Ion. I will go: but one thing in my fortune is lacking to me: if I shall not find her who bore me, my father, I cannot endure life: but, if I must utter a 670 prayer, may the woman who gave me birth be of Athens, that freedom of speech may be accorded to me through my mother. For if any alien's lot is cast in a city[1] *of* pure *race*, though he be in name a citizen, yet has he his mouth enslaved, and possesses not freedom to speak *his thoughts*.   675

Cho. Tears,* tears I see, and the woful beginnings of groans besides[2], when my royal mistress beholds her husband blessed with a son[3], and she is childless herself 680 and destitute of offspring. What a prophetic strain didst thou utter, O presaging son of Latona? whence, from whom of women, did this youth nurtured about thy temple, spring? For the response of the god not 685 pleases me, *as I am afraid* that it involves some deceit. I fear to what the event will come. For marvellous he 690 (i. e. apparently, Xuthus) reports *responses* marvellous to me, sounding well perhaps[4] to this *young man.* The youth bred of some other race has this good fortune by some deceit.[5] Who will not agree with me in this? Dear *sister slaves*, shall we tell *all* this distinctly to my 695 lady's ear about her husband, whose hopes *and fears*, poor *soul*, she used to share, having all *her affections bound up* in him[6]? But now she is overwhelmed with

---

1. Lit.—*For if any alien fall into a city.*
2. See note on 161.
3. Lit.—*Having child-blessedness.*
4. It seems impossible to make sense of τωδί ποτ᾽ εύφημα. I have substituted τάχα for πότε. This however is not satisfactory, and the passage appears hopelessly corrupt.
5. Lit.—*Has deceit and the fortune*—hendiadys, if the text is not corrupt, which is most probably the case.
6. In Greek it is more usual, when a participle and verb are combined in a clause, to put the participle first and construct the relative or other pronoun with it, leaving the pronoun to be understood with the verb. English idiom requires this to be reversed.

calamity, but he is fortunate,——*she* fallen into grey
700 age,[1] but her husband caring nought for his partner.[2]
Wretched man! who having come an alien to the
house, into great power and wealth,[3] has not preserved
consistency with his fortunes.   May he perish, may he
705 perish who has deceived my beloved mistress: and
may he not find favour when he offers at the fire the
cake sending forth its bright flame to the gods: but he
710 shall know me * * * * friend of the royal house.[4]
Already is approaching to the new-spread banquet the
son, and the new-found father.   O ye crags that
715 occupy the peaks and cloud-girt heights[5] of the rock
of Parnassus, where uplifting blazing torches, Bacchus
nimbly bounds with night-roaming Bacchanals.   Never[6]
720 may the youth come to my city, but may he quit his
young life and die.   For the city would have reason
in lamenting the entering in of strangers.   But enough,
enough *for as* King Erectheus that was our prince
before.

725   Cr.   O aged pedagogue[7] of Erectheus the father
that once was mine, when he was still in being,[8] ascend[9]

---

1. Hermann translates εἰσπεσοῦσα γῆρας by *quum consenuerit*,
and says such a use of the aorist is rare, but gives no other examples.
This usage is not very uncommon, when the main verb is future or
present with a really future sense.   But it can hardly be correct with
ἔρρει, which, though present, closely approximates in meaning
to a perfect.   We must not press the words too closely, especially as
the chorus may naturally be supposed to exaggerate a little; and then
the passage is plain enough.
2. Ἄτιετος φίλων—*Contemptor uxoris*.   Hermann.
3. Both included in ὄλβος.
4. Hermann supplies the lacuna by conjecture thus—τὸ δ' ἐμὸν
εἴσεται τᾶς χθονὸς ἀρχαίας (or τᾶς ἀπ' Ἐρεχθέως) ὅσον τυραννίδος φίλα.
This may be.
5. Lit.—*Abode*.
6. Lit.—*Never at all*.
7. For some account of the position and duties of a "pædagogus"
see Dict. of Antiq.
8. Lit.—*In light*.
9. Lit.—*Raise thyself* i. e. *come up the steps*.

to the oracle of the god, that thou mayest rejoice with
me, if King Loxias has spoken any oracle purporting[1]
the birth of children; for it is delightful to be pros- 730
perous in the company of friends, and if any evil (but
may it not so prove) should befal, it is sweet to look
upon the face of a man that loves us. But thee
I cherish in a father's place, thy mistress though I am,
as thou too didst my father once.

PEDAGOGUE.

Daughter, thou preservest the worthy manners of 735
worthy parents, and hast not disgraced thy race,
ancient as it is, sprung from the soil itself.[2] Pull me
on, pull me on and lead me to the temple. The oracle
is high up in truth: but do thou, helping my limbs to
accomplish the task,[3] be physician of mine old age.   740

CR. Come along with me then: but be careful
where thou settest thy foot.

PED. See. My foot indeed is slow, but my will
is quick.

CR. And support thyself, with thy staff as thou
goest over the ground.[4]

---

1. Ἐς not *regarding*, but *to the purpose of*.
2. If the old reading is correct, which is very doubtful, we
certainly cannot take together τοὺς σοὺς αὐτόχθονας or any similar
words, but must put commas after σούς and παλαιούς; and then
I know of no better way of understanding ἐκγονους αὐτόχθονας than
that proposed by Barnes, viz. as = τοὺς ἐξ αὐτῆς τῆς χθονὸς γεγενη-
μένους, though this is violent.
3. Lit.—*Working out my limb with me*.
4. *Explora solum scipione circa te.* Hermann. The accusative
is that of *motion over* a place (Hel. 598). More fully βάκτρῳ ἐρείδου
(cf. Tro. 150. Hec. 66) στίβον πορευόμενος......The real difficulty
is rather in the epithet περιφερῆ than in the grammatical construction.
Paley.
   I am somewhat disposed to think that the words may be taken thus
——ἐρείδου (i. e. ἔρεικε σεαυτῷ) στίβον (i. e. βάσιν) περιφερῆ χθονός
βάκτρῳ——*support for thyself thy going ambient of the ground with
thy staff* i. e. *support thy footsteps with thy staff as they go over the*

PED. This too is *a* blind *guide,* when I cannot see.

745   CR. Thou hast well said: but do not give in to the toil.

PED. I will not do so then willingly, but I have no control over what is wanting to me.

CR. Ye women, faithful slaves of my loom and shuttle, inform me what luck my husband who is gone, has met with as to children,[1] for the sake

750 of whom we came: for if ye shall declare good *news* to me, thou[2] wilt not confer joys on a mistress[3] *that will be* faithless *to reward you.*

CHO. O fate !

PED. The prelude to your words is not fortunate.

CHO. Ah ! wretched.

755   PED. But is there aught should grieve me in the response given to my lord ?[4]

CHO. Well. What are we to do *about* a matter about which death is *the* appointed *penalty ?*

CR. What strain is this, and about what are your fears ?

CHO. Shall we tell her, or be silent, or what shall we do ?

CR. Tell me; as thou knowest some calamity affecting me.

---

ground. Though this is not the ordinary meaning of ἐρείδομαι, it is strictly in analogy. But even taking ἐρείδου in its usual sense and regarding στίβου as a kind of cognate accus., as Paley suggests, I must at least strongly contend for the meaning I have assigned to περιφερῆ στίβου χθόνος.

1. Lit.—*Having received what luck of children my husband is gone.*

2. Addressed to the leader of the chorus.

3. Lit.—*Masters* i. e. *master and mistress,* but by the enallage of number here evidently referring to the latter only.

4. Lit.—*But am I aught distressed by the responses of my masters ?*

CHO. Told it shall be, even if I have to die twice 760
over. It is not granted to thee, my mistress, to take
children in thine arms, or ever draw them to thy
breast.

CR. Ah me! May I die!

PED. Daughter.

CR. Ah poor me for my calamity! I have
sustained, I have suffered, dear *handmaids*, a woe that
will not let me live.

PED. We are utterly undone, my daughter.   765

CR. Alas! alas! grief has stricken me through
and through to my heart.[1]

PED. Groan not yet—

CR. But *cause for* wailing is here.

PED. Before we learn—   770

CR. What news for me?

PED. If our master fares in like manner and is a
sharer in thy calamity, or thou art unhappy alone.

CHO. To him, old man, did Loxias grant a child,
and he is happy by himself without this lady.   775

CR. This evil upon evil[2] hast thou uttered, hast
thou uttered, a crowning grief for me to mourn.

PED. But is the child whom thou sayest, to
be begotten of some woman, or did he speak in the
oracle of one *already* born?

CHO. Loxias gives him *for a son* one that is 780
already a grown up young man: and I was present
when he received him.

CR. How sayest thou? Thou speakest words too
shocking to my ears[3] to be told, too shocking to
be told, too sad to utter.

---

1. Lit.—*Within these lungs.*
2. Lit.—*Upon this.*
3. The ethical dative ἐμοί.

PED.   Yes, and to mine also.   But tell me more
785 particularly how the oracle is fulfilled, and who
the youth is.

CHO.   Him whom thy husband should meet first
after departing from the god, the god gave to him for
a son.

CR.   Welladay! and I have gotten, have gotten
for my portion a life *all* childless, childless, and
790 in solitude shall inhabit a desolate home.

PED.   Who then *was it that* was spoken of by the
oracle?   Whom did the husband of the poor *lady*
meet?[1] and how, where did he see him?

CHO.   Knowest thou, my dear mistress, the young
795 man who was wont to sweep this temple?   This is the
youth.

CR.   O that I might fly through the humid air
afar from the Hellenic land up to the western
stars, such[2] *woe*, such[2] woe have I suffered, dear
handmaids.

800   PED.   And knowest thou *by* what name his father
calls him, or does this rest in silence not *yet* determined?

CHO.   Ion, as he was the first to meet his father.

PED.   And by what mother is he?

CHO.   I am not able to say.   But (that thou
mayst know all, old man, so far as I can tell thee[3]) the
husband of this lady is gone by stealth to the holy
805 house to offer for his son hospitable and natal

---

1.   Lit.—*To whom did the husband of the poor woman join the step
of his foot?*
2.   Lit—*Of what sort.* The Gr., and Engl. and Lat. idioms differ
in such expressions.   Engl. and Lat. express the antecedent words,
omit the relative: Greek expresses the relative words, omits the
antecedent.
3.   Lit.—*According to the things which are in my case.*

sacrifices,[1] and to join *in* a banquet along with his new-found son.

PED. My mistress, we are betrayed (for with thee do I suffer) by thy husband, and of set purpose are we outraged, and cast out from the house of Erectheus. 810 And I say it, not because I hate thy husband, but because I love thee more than him. For, when he[2] had wed thee, though he came into the city and into thy house a stranger, and had received all thy inheritance, he is proved to have stealthily begotten children 815 by some other woman: and how he stealthily *did so*, I will tell thee. When he found thee childless, he was not content to be like thee and to bear an equal *share* of *this* fate, but taking a servile partner, he lay with her secretly and begot the boy, and sending him out of 820 the country, gives him to one of the Delphians to rear: and he is nurtured holy-free[3] in the abode of the god, that he might remain unknown. But when he knew that he had grown up *to be* a young man, he persuaded thee to come hither on account of thy being childless. So then *it was* not the god *who* spoke falsely, but this 825 *thy husband who* spoke falsely, having long reared up[4] the boy, and fabricated *some* such web *of deceit* as this: if detected, he was ready to lay the blame[5] on the deity, but if he came *home with him*, wishing that lapse of time also would speak in its own defence,[6] he intended to invest him with the sovereignty of the land.

1. Apparently *sacrifices to celebrate Ion's admission into his house and Ion's birth*.
2. Lit.—*Who*.
3. See Paley's note on ἄφετος.
4. Lit.—*Long ago rearing up*—the Greek, Latin and French idiom, but not the English.
5. See note on 231.
6. This is nearly, if not quite, nonsense. The passage seems hopelessly corrupt. See Hermann and Paley.

830 And new is the name, devised for him after a long
course of time[1], Ion, because, I suppose, he met him as
he was going.

　　Cho.　Ah me! how I always detest wicked men,
who contrive acts of injustice, and then cloak them by
835 their devices.　I had rather get a dull honest man for
my friend than a bad man of quicker wit.

　　Ped.　And thou wilt suffer, *if he has his will,*
that which is the crowning evil of all these, introducing
into thine house, as its *future* lord, one who knows no
mother, who is of no account, *and born* of some woman
that is a slave.[2]　For the evil would have been single
840 *in its kind,* if pleading thy childlessness, he had
persuaded thee, and supplemented[3] his house from a
well-born mother: but if this was grievous to thee,
he should have sought a union with some descendant
of Æolus[4].　After this thou must now do some deed
worthy of a woman: for thou *must* slay thy husband
845 and his son, either by taking a sword, or by some
plot, or by poison, before death befal thee by them:
for if thou shalt spare him, thou wilt be deprived of
life:[5] for when two enemies[6] come beneath one roof,
either the one[6] or the other[6] must suffer.

　　1.　*i. e.　Not his original name.* 'Ανὰ χρόνον cannot mean, as
Paley hesitatingly suggests, *according to the circumstances of the time.*
This would be ἀνὰ καῖρον.　'Ανὰ χρόνον is merely another expression
for χρόνιον.

　　2.　Paley cannot see why Hermann should prefer ἄγει to ἄγειν=
τὸ ἄγειν ἐκεῖνον, he says.　If this is to be the sense, I certainly with
Hermann prefer ἄγει, not because ἄγειν would in any way require the
article, but because after πείσει 2. pers. ἄγειν would naturally have a
subject in the 2. pers., unless ἐκεῖνον or its equivalent were expressed.
But I can see no objection to ἄγειν really, because this is no doubt
the true way of understanding the passage.

　　3.　Lit.—*Colonised, settled.*

　　4.　Lit.—*The nuptials of Æolus.*

　　5.　Lit.—*Depart from life.*

　　6.　Observe that these words are neuter.　Such neuters are used
especially in indefinite and general expressions.

I then am willing both to aid thee in accomplishing 850
the deed, and to go into the house where he is
making ready the banquet, and help to slay the youth,
and, if I but repay my mistress[1] for my nurture,
either[2] to die, or[2] to live and still behold the light.
For *there is* one thing *that* brings shame upon slaves,
the name: but in all else no slave, who is right- 855
minded, is worse than the free.

Cho.   I too, my beloved mistress, am willing to
share this calamity with thee, and either to die, or to
live, *if it be* with honour.

Cr.   O my soul, how shall I be silent? yet how
shall I reveal my clandestine loves and bid farewell to 860
shame? *And yet why should I not?* For what obstacle
is yet left to hinder me? With whom should[3] I now
engage in contests of virtue? Has not my husband
been a traitor to me? And I am bereft of home, bereft 865
of children, and gone are the hopes which I cherished
to arrange matters happily but failed,[4] by keeping my
loves secret, by keeping secret my deeply bewailed
child-bearing. But no, by[5] the starry dwelling of Jove, 870
and by the goddess of[6] my *native* rocks, and by the
hallowed shore of the watery Tritonian pool, no longer
will I conceal my loves, as I shall be relieved by un- 875
burdening my breast. My eyes drop with tears, and my
soul is sick, conspired against both by men, and by immortals, whom I will proclaim ungrateful betrayers of my 880
love. O thou that modulatest the voice of the seven-toned
harp, which utters forth the sweet melodies of song to

---

1. See note on 751.
2. Lit.—*Both......and.*
3. See note on 231.
4. Lit.—*The hopes, which seeking to arrange well, I was not able.*
5. On the omission of μά, see Paley's note.
6. Lit.—*At.*

shepherds on the dumb sounding-board, to thee, O son
885 of Latona, will I proclaim reproach before this light
of day. Thou camest to me, thy locks all glittering
with gold, when I was gathering into the bosom of
890 my robe the blooming crocus leaves of golden sheen:
and clinging to the white wrists of my hands, thou, a
god, leddest me, in spite of my *virgin* shame, crying
out " O mother, mother," into the chamber of a grot,
895 to lie with me, doing a pleasure to the Cyprian queen.
And I, ill-fated maid, bear to thee a boy, whom from
fear of my mother I place in *the grotto which thou
chosest for* thy couch, where thou didst embrace
900 hapless me in hapless intercourse, ill-fated maid:
(ah me! ah me!) and now to me is lost thy poor
boy, carried away as a feast for the birds, but thou
905 makest music with thy lyre, playing songs of joy.
Ho! to the son of Latona I speak, to thee who
grantest by lot[1] the divine voice *of prophecy;* before thy
910 golden shrine and dwelling in mid-earth, in thine ears
will I utter aloud my speech.   Ha! base seducer *that
thou art,* who, having received from him no favours to
915 repay,[2] art bringing a son to dwell in the house of my
husband; whilst my child and thine own[3] has perished
unnoticed, carried off by birds of prey, stripped of his
mother's swathing bands.[4]   Hates thee Delos, and the
920 branches of the laurel beside the delicate-leaved palm,
where Latona bore thee, her divine offspring, by
impregnation of Jove.

---

1. Those who would consult the god, cast lots for the order in
which they should receive responses.
2. The force of προ in προλαβών.
3. The force of γέ.
4. Lit.—*Having passed out of,* not, I think, *having exchanged
hem for others* (Paley's version)—for what could these *others* be?

Cho. Alas! how great a store of evils is being opened, at which any one might shed the tear.

Ped. Daughter, I cannot in truth look long 925 enough on thy face *to satisfy myself that this is not a dream*, and I am beside my senses. For as I was just getting rid of a wave of troubles in my mind,[1] another in the wake upheaves me, *raised* by thy words, in which,[2] no sooner hast thou spoken of the troubles *immediately* before thee, than thou hast gone off to a sad recital of other woes.[3] What sayest thou? what 930 charge bringest thou against Loxias? what son *is this* thou sayest thou didst bear? where placedst him in the city, to be entombed as a sweet meal in the bowels of wild beasts?[4] Repeat it to me again.

Cr. I feel abashed before thee, old man, but nathless I will tell it.

Ped. Ay, for I know how to mourn in generous 935 sympathy with friends.

Cr. Hear then : thou knowest the cavern on the north side of the Cecropian rock,[5] which we call the Macræ?[6]

Ped. I know it, where there are a shrine and altars of Pan close by.

Cr. Here I went through[7] a terrible struggle.

---

1. This sentence is an instance of anacoluthon, the construction in this line, nominative, being changed in the next to the accusative.
2. See note on 697.
3. Lit.—*Thou hast by a change gone the sad direction of other woes.* See Paley's note on the genitive τῶν παρ. κακῶν in the preceding line.
4. Lit.—*An entombed thing dear to the wild beasts.*
5. i.e. *The Acropolis.*
6. This is spoken in a loose sense. Strictly speaking the cavern was not called Macræ, but the rocks in which it was situated.
7. Ἠγωνίσμεθα, must here be pluperf., not perf. Engl. idiom requires that it should be translated as an aor., which would be the more usual tense in Greek.

940   PED. What *struggle? Say*, for my tears rise at thy words.[1]

CR. I contracted a hapless intercourse with Phœbus against my will.

PED. Daughter, was this then what I heard of?

CR. I know not: but if thou *art* right *in what thou* speakest of, I will confess it.

PED. When thou wast suffering in secret from *some* concealed malady?

945   CR. Then *it was that* the evil happened which I now plainly declare to thee.

PED. And after—how didst thou conceal thy amours with Phœbus?

CR. I bore a child: endure to hear this from me, aged man.

PED. Who delivers thee? *and* where? Or dost thou go through these sufferings *all* alone?

CR. Alone, in the very[2] cavern where I was embraced *by the god*.

950   PED. But where is the child? *Say*, that no longer childless thou mayest be.

CR. He is dead, old man, having been exposed to the wild beasts.

PED. Dead? And did that base Apollo in no way aid him?

CR. He aided him not, but he is spending his boyhood in Hades.

PED. Why, who exposed him? For surely thou didst not.

955   CR. I did, in the darkness, swathing him with my robe.

---

1. Lit.—*Since tears meet for me thy words.*
2. The περ in οὖπερ.

PED. And did none aid thee in exposing the child?

CR. None beside my misfortunes and *the necessity for* concealment.[1]

PED. And how hadst thou the heart to leave thy child in the cavern?

CR. How? *I left him* after uttering many piteous words from my mouth.

PED. Alas! hard-hearted thou for the deed, but 960 more than thou the god.

CR. Yes, hadst thou seen the boy stretching out his hands to me.

PED. Seeking the breast, or to lie in thy arms?

CR. In them, from which it was cruel of me to keep him.[2]

PED. But how came it into thy mind to expose the child?

CR. I thought that the god would preserve his 965 own son.[3]

PED. Ah me! How is the prosperity of thy house destroyed by storms.

---

1. Paley corrects Dr. Badham's translation "Calamity and concealment were my only witnesses," on which his own version is undoubtedly a considerable improvement; but he seems to have mistaken the meaning of τὸ λανθάνειν.

2. Lit.—*There, where being not he was suffering unjust things from me.*

3. On this and the preceding line, Paley has the following note:—

"'Ες τί δόξης ἦλθέ σοι for σὺ δὲ πῶς ἐς δόξαν ἦλθες. Hermann gives σοὶ δ' ἐς τί δόξ' εἰσῆλθεν. With the following ὡς supply ἐξέβαλον ὡς νομίζουσα &c. See Rhes. 145. The old reading σώζοντα was corrected by several critics."

About the general meaning of the passage there cannot be two opinions. But this is rather special pleading. I must confess I prefer Hermann's reading. Or I should like still better—σὺ δ' ἐς τί δόξης ἦλθες ἐκβαλὼν τέκνον; but *what didst thou expect, when thou hadst exposed the child?*—to which the answer is (ἐς τὴν δόξαν ἦλθον) ὡς τὸν θεὸν σώσοντα &c. (*I expected*) *that the god would preserve &c.*

CR. Why dost thou hide thy head, old man, and shed tears?

PED. Because I see thee and thy father[1] involved in misfortunes.

CR. Such are human affairs: nothing remains constant.

970 PED. Let us therefore, daughter, no longer go on lamenting.[2]

CR. Why, what must I do? To be in misfortunes is to be helpless.[3]

PED. Requite the god who was the first to do thee wrong.

CR. And how am I, mortal as I am, to overcome[4] mightier beings?

PED. Fire the holy oracle of Loxias.

975 CR. I am afraid: even now I have woes enough.

PED. Dare then what thou canst do—to slay thy husband.

CR. I cannot do it, for the sake of our wedded life[5] in those days when he was faithful.

PED. But do thou at least[6] *slay* the youth who has appeared *as a usurper* over thee.

CR. How? O that it were possible! For[7] I should be glad *to do it*.

980 PED. By arming thy attendants with swords.[8]

CR. I will go *and do so*; but where shall this be done?

---

1. See Paley's note.
2. Lit.—*Stick to lamentations.*
3. Lit.—*A fix*, for this vulgar English word expresses it exactly.
4. I think Paley is mistaken in supposing ὑπερδραμεῖν to mean *escape from punishment* in this passage. For, if so, where is the connexion in sense between this line and the following one?
5. Lit.—*I reverence our wedded life.*
6. For ἀλλά, compare line 426.
7. Lit.—*Since.*
8. Ξιφηφόρους appears, preferably, proleptic in sense.

PED. In the sacred tent, where he is feasting his friends.

CR. The slaying *of him thus* is an undisguised deed, and my slaves are weak *to protect me.*

PED. Alas! thou art turning coward. Come, do thou then propose something.

CR. Well, I have *a plan to kill him* by guile and 985 *a plan* to act.¹

PED. In either² of these will I be thy helper.

CR. Hear then: thou knowest about the battle of the sons of Earth?

PED. I do, the battle which the Giants waged with the gods at Phlegra.

CR. There Earth brought forth the Gorgon, terrible monster.

PED. As an ally to her children *and* foe of the 990 gods?³

CR. Yes: and the daughter of Jupiter, the goddess Pallas, slew her.

PED. What sort of savage appearance had she?

CR. *She had* a breast-plate armed with the coils of a hydra.

PED. Is this the story which I have long ago heard?

CR. That *it is* her hide *which* Minerva wears on 995 her breast.

PED. What they call the ægis, the accoutrement of Pallas?

---

1. I have endeavoured to preserve the "double entente." Δραστήρια means either *active, effectual,* the sense intended by Creusa—δόλια καὶ δραστήρια, *a plan to kill him by guile, and that an efficacious one,*—or *accomplished by action,* the sense in which the pedagogue (as appears from the next line) understood her—*a plan to kill him by guile, and another plan to kill him by violence.*
2. Lit.—*Both.*
3. Θεῶν πόνον i. e. θεοῖς πόνους παρέξουσαν.

CR. It got this name, when she came to the wars[1] of the gods.

PED. What harm, I pray, is this to thy enemies, my daughter?

CR. Knowest thou Erichthonius, or not? But how canst thou fail to know him,[2] old man?

1000 PED. Him, whom the earth produced, the first ancestor of your race?[3]

CR. To him, when new-born, Pallas gives—

PED. What? For thou art saying something which excites my expectation.[4]

CR. Two drops from the blood of the Gorgon—

PED. And what virtue should it have against the life[5] of a man?

1005 CR. One of them causing death, and the other able to heal diseases.

PED. By what did she attach it to the boy's body?[6]

CR. By a band of gold: and he gives it to my father.

PED. And, when he died, it came to thee?

CR. Yes: and I wear it on the wrist of my hand.

1010 PED. How then is the two-fold gift of the goddess made effectual?[7]

CR. That which[8] dropped from the gore of the hollow vein—

---

1. Lit.—*Spear.* Paley observes—" He probably means that the ægis now first obtained its name from ἀίσσειν, not from αἴξ."

2. Lit.—*But why art thou not likely (to know him)?*

3. Lit.—*Of you.*

4. Unusual as such a meaning may be, I am inclined to think Paley is right in the interpretation of μέλλον.

5. Lit.—*Nature, constitution.*

6. Lit.—*Attach it about the boy from his body.*

7. Lit.—*Effected.*

8. Ὅστις—sc. σταλαγμός. If the vulgate text be right, this is one of the very few passages where ὅστις is a synonym of ὅς. Paley. The Gorgon's head was cut off.

PED.   For what purpose is this to be used?[1]
What virtue does it exert?

CR.   It wards off diseases and has the power of
supporting life.

PED.   But the second[2] which thou speakest of,
what does it?

CR.   It kills, being the venom of the Gorgon's 1015
snakes.

PED.   And dost thou bear it mingled in one,
or separately?

CR.   Separately: for good mixes not with evil.

PED.   My dearest daughter, all hast thou which
thou needest.

CR.   By this the youth shall die: and thou shalt
be his slayer.

PED.   Where? And what shall I do?[3] 'Tis thine 1020
to speak, and mine to dare.

CR.   In Athens, when he comes to my house.

PED.   This hast thou not well said: *forgive my
words*, for thou too findest fault with my *plan*.

CR.   How *not well said?* Hast thou suspected
that which *now* occurs to me also?

PED.   Thou wilt appear to have slain the boy,
even if thou shalt not kill him.

CR.   Right: for they say that stepmothers bear 1025
enmity to children.

PED.   Kill him therefore here,[4] that thou mayst
be able to deny the murder.

---

1. Lit.—Τί τῷδε χρῆσθαι sc. δεῖ; Lit.—*What (use) does it behove
to use this?*
2. Lit.—*The second number*, much like the English *number
two.*
3. Lit.—*Having done what?*
4. Lit.—*At the place itself.*

CR.   Ay, and I enjoy the pleasure of slaying him so much the earlier.[1]

PED.   And thou wilt not be known to thy husband *to possess* the secret which he is anxious should not be known to thee.[2]

CR.   Knowest thou then what thou art to do? 1030   Take from my hand this gold bracelet of Minerva's, an antique work, go where my husband by stealth is banqueting on the slain ox,[3] and when they cease from the feast and are about to pour libations to the gods, keeping this *concealed* in thy robe, drop[4] *the contents* into the young man's cup (but *into his* 1035   individually, not *the cups* of all, distinguishing his draught *from the rest*[5]) who is about to lord it over my house. And if it *once* pass his throat, never will he come to renowned Athens, but will die and abide here.

PED.   Do thou then depart[6] to the house of our 1040   hosts;[7] and I will perform *the task* to which I am appointed. Come, aged foot, grow young for work, though it is not natural to thee from *long course of* time. And go with my mistress[8] against a foe,

---

1. Lit.—*I take (a portion) of the pleasure earlier by the (amount of) time*—ἡδονῆς partitive gen., χρόνῳ dat. of measure of excess. Paley gives another explanation; but I have no doubt this is the true interpretation of the passage.
2. This is Hermann's interpretation—"Latebit maritum tuum, scire te, quæ ille te latere cupit." Paley follows. It is not easy to get this sense out of the Greek, and when got, it is not very much to the purpose, however ingeniously Hermann has explained the motive for Creusa's concealing her knowledge of Ion's parentage. Conjectural criticism is rather out of fashion; but I cannot help believing that Euripides wrote—καὶ σόν γε λήσεις πόσιν ἃ σὺ σπεύδεις λαθεῖν.
3. Compare 664. Ἡμῖν—ethical dative.
4. Lit.—*Drop having thrown.*
5. The reasons for rejecting this line may be seen in Paley's note. To say the least, it comes in very awkwardly.
6. Lit.—*Transfer thy foot.*
7. The πρόξενοι were public entertainers whose duty it was to lodge visitors to Delphi.
8. See note on 852.

and help to slay him and to rid her house of him.[1]
For it is a fine thing for men in prosperity to hold 1045
righteousness in honour, but when any one would
work harm to enemies, there is no law laid down
to forbid it.

Cho. Enodia,[2] daughter of Ceres, who art queen
of nightly visitants,[3] guide also in the light of day the 1050
contents of the fatal bowl to them for whom my loved,
loved mistress sends it, *contents taken* from the drops
trickling from the wounded throat of earth-born 1055
Gorgon, to him who aspires to the house of the
Erecthidæ.[4] Nor may any other of another house
ever reign over the city besides the noble Erecthidæ. 1060
But if his death shall fail to be accomplished, and the
eager schemes of our mistress, and the opportunity
for the daring deed shall pass away, by which her
hopes are now sustained,[5] either she will take[6] a
sharpened sword, or she will fasten a noose to 1065
her throat about her neck, and putting an end to her
sufferings by sufferings, she will go down to another
form of life.[7] For never would she live and endure
in *the sight of* her brightly beaming eyes[8] others of 1070
alien race ruling her house,—she that is born of
so noble a line as hers.[9] I feel shame for the god of

---

1. Lit.—*Jointly remove him from the house.*
2. i.e. *Goddess of the roads*, Lat. *Trivia.* Hecate is here invoked, as presiding over poisons. In making her the daughter of Ceres, Euripides confounds here with Proserpine.
3. i.e. *Apparitions.*
4. Paley's interpretation of this passage seems the only right one.
5. Φέρετ' i.e. φέρεται. See Paley's note.
6. By a zeugma, ἐξάψει in the following line is used with ξίφος as well as its proper object βρόχον.
7. Viz. *in Hades.*
8. Lit.—*The bright splendours of her eyes.*
9. This seems to be the force of τῶν—*of the noble line (of which she comes).*

E

1075 many hymns,[1] if keeping vigil he shall in the night
     behold[2] the torch that witnesses the Icades about the
     springs of Callichorus,[3] when the star-eyed heavens of
1080 Jove too wont to dance, and dances the Moon, and
     the fifty daughters of Nereus, who dance over the sea
1085 and the eddies of ever flowing-streams, in honour of
     the Daughter[4] with the golden crown and the
     hallowed Mother;[4] where, entering on the possessions
1090 of others, the homeless foster-child of Phœbus[5] hopes
     to reign.   All ye who, following after poesy, sing in
     reproachful strains our loves and unlawful unholy
     alliances *coming* of the Cyprian queen, see how much
1095 we surpass in purity the unrighteous race of men.
     Let the contrary song go forth against men, and
     the verse reproachful for[6] their amours.   For the
1100 descendant from the sons of Jove shews his forgetful-
     ness *of her* in not begetting for my mistress·children
     who should be a boon common to the house:[7] but
1105 instead of this, to please Venus,[8] he has gotten him
     a bastard son.

          ATTENDANT.   Stranger women,[9] where shall I find

---

1. Bacchus, who was escorted with a solemn torch-procession
from Athens to Eleusis on the twentieth day of Boedromion, whence
the whole nine days' festival is called εἰκάδες (εἴκοσι). The *hymns* are
specially the dithyrambs.

2. i.e. *He, viz. Ion, shall ever be allowed to behold, though his
mother was,* as supposed, *a slave.*

3. A spring near Eleusis.

4. i.e. *Proserpine and Ceres,* worshipped under these special
names at Athens. These accusatives seem to depend on χορεύει above
in the sense of *celebrates in dances.*

5. Lit.—*The Phœbean wanderer.*

6. Lit.—*About.*

7. Lit.—*Not having begotten for my mistress the luck of children
common to the house.*

8. Lit.—*Having laid up in store for himself an obligation.* Paley
seems to me to misunderstand ἄλλαν. It is best taken in agreement
with 'Αφροδίταν, in a corresponding sense to that of ἄλλος in 161,
where see note.

9. i.e. *Strangers to Delphi.*

my mistress the daughter of Erectheus? For I have gone all over the city seeking her,[1] and am not able to find her.

CHO. But what is the matter, my fellow-slave? What makes thy feet in such eager haste?[2] and what tidings dost thou bring?

ATT. We are pursued; and the native magistrates of the land are in search of her, that she may be stoned to death.

CHO. Alas! What wilt thou say? Surely we have not been discovered in contriving a secret murder against the youth?

ATT. Thou art right:[3] and thou wilt be not amongst the last to share in the evil consequences.

CHO. But how was the secret plot discovered?

ATT. The god, not willing to be defiled, found out a way for unrighteousness to be overcome of right.

CHO. How? I pray and beseech thee[4] to tell me this. For we should die more contentedly, when we have learned whether we must die or still behold the light.[5]

ATT. When the husband of Creusa, having left the oracle of the god, and having received his new son, had gone away to the banquet and offerings which he was preparing in honour of the gods,

---

1. Lit. *For seeking her in every direction of the city I have completed (the round of) it.*
2. Lit.—*What eagerness of feet possesses thee?*
3. Lit.—*Thou hast known.*
4. Lit.—*A suppliant I beseech thee.*
5. I follow Paley's punctuation and the translation implied in his note. But the εἶθ' ὁρᾶν φάος is sadly in the way. I much prefer Hermann's comma after πεπυσμέναι, the meaning, I think, being— *For when we have learned this, if we must needs die, we shall die more contentedly, and, if we are to live, (we shall be able to rest, which we cannot now do for curiosity).*

1125 Xuthus himself[1] went where the fire of the god
bounds in Bacchic dance,[2] that he might steep the
twin rocks in *the blood of* sacrifices to Bacchus in the
place of his son's opteria,[3] first saying to him:
Do thou then, my son, stay and rear a spacious[4] tent
1130 by the labours of artificers. But if I stay a long time
in sacrificing[5] to the gods presiding over birth, let
there be a feast for thy assembled friends. And
taking the calves, he went his way. But the young
man in due form proceeded to erect the unwalled
1135 enclosure of the tent with upright poles, carefully
guarding neither towards the mid-day[6] beams of the
sun's fires *to erect it*, nor on the other hand towards
his dying rays, *and* measuring out a plethrum's
length square (*a space of ground* having[7] *for* the
contents of its area a sum of ten thousand feet, as say
1140 those skilled *in numbers*), with intent to invite
all the people of Delphi to the feast. And having
gotten sacred hangings from the treasury *of the
temple*, works wondrously beautiful for men to behold,
he made *with them* a covering *for the tent*. First he

---

1. In the Greek, Ξοῦθος μέν is opposed to ὁ δὲ νεανίας in 1132—
Xuthus on the one hand......the youth on the other hand. We may
get this sense virtually in English by saying *Xuthus Himself.*
2. The two peaks of Parnassus were sacred to Apollo and Bacchus
respectively, and on one lights were said to be seen, which were
attributed to the torch-light dances of Bacchus and the nymphs.
3. This festival (on occasion of a child's being shewn to the
friends of the parents on the eighth or ninth day) had not of course
been celebrated at the proper time in Ion's case.
4. See Paley's note on the proper meaning of ἀμφήρης.
5. Θύσας—*Having begun to sacrifice*, and therefore here virtually=
Θύων. This use of the aorist participle, in itself remarkable enough,
is common in such expressions as βασιλεύσας, *having begun to
reign &c.*
6. Lit.—*Middle.*
7. I have pushed in γῆν for ἔχουσαν to agree with, though of
course this cannot be. The two lines 1138, 1139, are either corrupt,
or, as Paley says, a downright interpolation.

spreads over the roof a dependent awning[1] of pepli,
the offering of the son of Jove, which Hercules
presented to the god as the spoils of the Amazons. 1145
And there was[2] woven in them in pictured forms
a design[3] of this kind: Uranus[4] marshalling the
heavenly bodies in the circle of the sky. The
Sun was urging his horses towards his last fires,
ushering in the bright light of Hesperus. And
dark-robed Night was whirling her car with a yoke of 1150
two steeds:[5] and the stars were bearing the goddess
company. The Pleiad was going through the
mid sky, and Orion girt with sword: and above, the
Bear wheeling round her tail-stars by *the revolution of*
the golden pole. And the orb of the full moon 1155
dividing the month in the midst was shooting upward,
and the Hyades, most certain token for mariners, and
the light-bringing Aurora chasing *away* the stars.
And on the walls[6] he hung other works of bar-
barian looms,[7] well-rowed ships opposed to Grecian 1160
ships, and wights, half men, half beasts, and
their huntings *on* horses'[8] *feet*, the chase of stags and

---

1. An awning laid across the ridge and falling upon the slanting
roof on either side, would appropriately be called πτέρυξ, as
resembling the drooping pinions of a bird. Paley.
2. Paley remarks that this usage, where a verb, placed before a
plur. masc. or fem., is itself in the singular number, is rare in Attic
Greek; but he quotes other instances in Pers. 49. Trachin. 520.
Bacch. 1350, Hel. 1358.
3. Lit.—*Weavings.*
4. i. e. A personification of the heavens.
5. When there were two horses to a chariot, they were attached
to the pole by a yoke. Any beyond this number were harnessed on
each side of the yoke-horses by traces. 'Ασείρωτον ὄχημα is therefore
a chariot without such additional horses.
6. i. e. *Sides.*
7. Lit.—*Other webs of barbarians.*
8. I cannot but think Paley wrong in supposing that ἱππείας
ἄγρας alludes to the capture of the Thracian Diomede's mares by
Hercules. It is much more natural to give it an active sense, and

fierce lions, and at the entrance, Cecrops beside
his daughters coiling *himself* in folds,[1] the offering of
1165 one of the Athenians: and in the midst of the feast
he set goblets of gold; and a herald standing
on tip-toe proclaimed that any inhabitant of the city
who would was to come to the banquet. But when
the tent was filled, adorned with garlands they
1170 satisfied their appetite with abundant food. And
when they had ceased from the enjoyment of it,
an old man * came forward and stood in the midst,[2]
and caused great laughter to the guests by his zealous
activity:[3] for he sent *round* water from the water-
pots to wash their hands,[4] and burned the gum
1175 of myrrh, and took charge of the gold vessels of
libation, of his own accord setting himself this task.
And when they came to the flutes and to the common
bowl, the old man said, Ye must take away the
small wine-cups, and bring in large ones, that
1180 *the guests* who are present may more quickly make
their hearts merry.[5] Forthwith[6] there was a bustle
of *attendants* bringing silver-wrought pateræ and
golden: and he, taking a vessel selected *from the rest*,
as if forsooth to do a pleasure to the new lord, offered
1185 it to him full, having *first* put into the wine an active
poison which they say our mistress gave him, that the

take it in apposition with θηράματα, as there is no connecting word
after ἐλάφων. I may be wrong in considering it involves a kind of
supplementary description of the Centaurs (they have been called
φῶτες, and now are ἵπποι), but the connexion in which the words
occur, is at least an apology for this idea.
1. Cecrops was represented in statues with the tail of a serpent
instead of legs and feet.
2. Lit.—*Having come forward into the middle ground.*
3. Lit.—*Doing zealous things.*
4. Lit.—*As washings for their hands.*
5. Lit.—*Come to delights of their minds.*
6. Δή.

young man might quit the light : and none knew[1] of
this : but whilst the new-found son amongst the rest
was holding the libation[2] in his hands, one of the
slaves spoke an unlucky word: and he, as being 1190
brought up in the temple and amongst holy sooth-
sayers, deemed it an omen, and bade fill a fresh
bowl : and the first libation intended for the god[3]
he throws to the ground, and tells all to empty *their*
paterœ. And silence came over them. And we fill
the sacred bowls with liquor and Byblian juice. 1195
And in the midst of this act a winged company
of doves alights in the tent; for in the house
of Loxias they dwell without fear. And when they
had poured away the wine, they, in want of drink,
dipped their beaks into it, and drew it into their 1200
feathered throats. And to the rest of them the
intended libation to the god was harmless : but the
one which had settled[4] where the new-found son had
poured *out his cup,* and had tasted the liquor, anon
shewed her plumed body convulsed,[5] and became wild
as a bacchanal, and screaming uttered sounds unac-
countable : and all the company of banqueters 1205
marvelled at the sufferings[6] of the bird : and she
dies heaving convulsively, stretching[7] out her red
claws. But the predicted son dashed forth his bare
arms[8] from his robe across the table, and shouts,

---

1. For ᾔδειν 3 pers., see Paley's note.
2. Lit.—*But for the son who had appeared, holding with others*
the libation. Παιδί is dat. of disadvantage. We lose the precise force
in the English.
3. Lit.—*The before libations of the god.*
4. Lit.—*Was sitting.*
5. Lit.—*Shook her plumed body.*
6. I am not sure that it is not rather *actions,* like the vulgar
English (as it now is) *works.* On θάμβησεν without augm. see
Paley's note.
7. Lit.—*Having relaxed.*
8. Lit.—*Limbs.*

1210 Who of men intended to kill me? Shew me, old
man : for thine was the officious zeal *that served me*,
and from thy hand I received the draught. And
immediately he seizes his aged arm and searches him,
that he might catch the old man in the fact in
1215 possession *of the poison*. And he was discovered,
and then he was with difficulty compelled to reveal[1]
the attempt of Creusa and the plot of the draught
of wine. And the youth who had been made known
by the oracle of Loxias,[2] rushes out, taking the
banqueters with him, and standing before the Pythian
1220 rulers, he says, O sacred land! An attempt is made
to murder me[3] with poison by the daughter of
Erectheus, a stranger woman. And the princes[3]
of Delphi decreed by general vote[4] that my mistress
should die by being hurled from a rock, as plotting
to kill[5] him that is consecrated, and attempting to
1225 enact[5] a murder in the temple. And all the city
is seeking her who with wretched fate pursued
her wretched journey *hither* : for having come *hither*
to ask children[6] from Phœbus, she has lost her life[7]
along with *the hope of* offspring.

CHO. No *way* there is, no way for hapless
1230 me there is to escape from death : for discovered now,
discovered are these schemes of a libation from the
clusters of Bacchus mingled with death by *the infusion*

---

1. Lit.—*Having been compelled, he revealed*.
2. Lit.—*The youth Pythian-oracle-declared of Loxias*.
3. Probably the same as the ἀριστῆς of 416.
4. Lit.—*By not one vote (only)*—a litotes to signify *by their unanimous votes*.
5. See note on 231.
6. Lit.—*To the desire of children*.
7. Lit.—*Body*.

of the swiftly working drops *of the* hydra's *blood*,[1]
discovered is the *purposed* sacrifice to the gods
below,—a discovery putting an end to my life, and 1235
bringing the penalty on my mistress of being stoned
to death.[2] Whither shall I flee[3] with wings or under
the dark depths of the earth, to escape the calamity
of death by stoning? Shall I mount a chariot with four 1240
steeds of fleetest hoof, or the poop of ship?[4] It is not
possible to escape detection, when the god desires not
to screen us from the penalty of crime.[5] What *fate*
awaits thee, O my poor mistress, to suffer bodily?[6] 1245
Shall we, before we suffer, determine to do some
mischief to others[7] ourselves, as is *but* just?

Cr. My handmaids, I am pursued to be put
to death, condemned[8] by the Pythian vote, and I am
on the point of being given up *to justice.*

Cho. We know thy misfortunes, O wretched 1250
lady, in what a *sad* condition thou art.

Cr. Whither then shall I fly? For with diffi-

---

1. This seems to be better than Paley's way of taking the passage,
both on general grounds, and because φόνος seems a strange word to
apply to the death of the dove.
2. Lit.—*A misfortune to my life, and a stony death to my mistress,*
συμφοραί being in apposition not with one word, but all the former
part of the sentence. In the previous ῥῆσις Creusa was to die
πετρορριφής, which may either mean *by hurling from a rock,* or *by
being stoned.* The former was the meaning intended, as we find
by-and-by, but the Chorus seems to have understood it in the latter
sense.
3. Lit.—*What flight shall I go?*
4. Lit.—*Having mounted the swiftest hoof of four-horse chariots,
or the poops on ships?* The construction is rather involved, and the
expression forced. Why not read—τεθρ. ὠκίσταν χαλᾶν (all gen.)
ἐπιβᾶσ', ἢ πρύμνας ἐπι ναῶν—?
5. A general proposition. Lit.—*When the god does not get us
off stealthily, desiring it.*
6. Lit.—*In thy life.*
7. Lit.—*Shall we suffer, choosing to do some mischief to our
neighbours?*
8. Lit.—*For fatal slaughter, having been overcome.* On the sing.
κρατηθεῖσα after the pl. διωκόμεσθα, see Paley.

culty have I avoided death by getting the start of my pursuers in rushing from the house,[1] and *it is only* by stealth, by eluding my enemies, that I have come here.

Cho. And whither else shouldest thou *fly* but to the altar ?

Cr. And what will this avail me ?[2]

Cho. The gods permit not to slay a suppliant.

Cr. Yes, but *it is* by the law *that* I am to die.

1255   Cho. Yes, if thou shouldst be taken and shouldst be in their power.[3]

Cr. Ay, and here come on apace towards us[4] my bitter enemies sword in hand.

Cho. Sit therefore at the altar. For even if thou shouldst be slain whilst thou art there, thou wilt entail on those who kill thee blood demanding vengeance : but we must bear our lot.

Ion. O bull-faced visage of Cephisus her fore-

1260 father, what a viper *is* this *that* thou hast begotten, or *rather* dragon with eyes flashing murderous flames of fire,[5] in whom is all daring, nor is she less cruel[6] than the drops of Gorgon's *blood*, with which she sought

1265 to kill me. Seize her, that the summit of Parnassus, whence she shall be hurled *by* a bound from the rock, may cause those unsullied locks of hers to be torn.[7] But a good fortune was mine, that prevented me from going[8] to the city of Athens and falling under

---

1. Paley's explanation is excellent—ἔφθασα πόδα ὑπεξάγουσα (ἐξ οἴκων), ὥστε μὴ θανεῖν.
2. Lit.—*And what more is this to me ?*
3. Lit.—*Having been taken in their power.* Χειρία is proleptic.
4. Lit.—*Hither.*
5. Lit.—*Looking up or back the murderous flame of fire.*
6. Lit.—*Less.*
7. Lit.—*May card thoroughly the unsullied locks of her.*
8. Lit.—*But a good deity I met with, before I went &c.*

the power of a step-mother. For amongst those who 1270
have befriended me do I reckon[1] thy disposition
towards me, in that thou wast a spite and a foe to
me: for if thou hadst *once* entrapped me in thy
house, thou wouldst have sent me outright to the
mansions of Hades. But neither will the altar nor
the temple of Apollo save thee, and any feeling of
pity for thee is outweighed by pity for me and for
my mother:[2] for though her bodily presence is 1275
wanting to me, yet thus far is not the name of a
mother wanting.[3] See what scheme after scheme
this vile woman[4] has contrived: she has *now* crouched
down at the altar, thinking to escape from the
punishment due to her deeds.

Cr. I warn thee not to slay me where I have 1280
stationed myself, both for my sake and the god's.

Ion. And what hast thou to do with Phœbus?[5]

Cr. I commit my body as sacred to the keeping
of the god.[6]

Ion. And yet thou didst try to slay the child of
the god with poison.

Cr. But thou wast no longer the child of 1285
Loxias, but thy own father's.

Ion. But I was, I mean *in* the absence of
my father.

---

1. The aorist here has much the same sense as a perfect—*I have
reckoned and do reckon still.* So εἶπον in Med. 274 (Pors.)
2. Lit.—*And the pity that is thine is present* i. e. *is accorded
stronger to me and to my mother.* The meaning of the passage seems
to be that the general feeling of pity for him and for his mother
was so strong, that none would connive at Creusa's escape from the
altar, or aid her whilst she remained there.
3. This seems to mean—*As yet there is no reason to disbelieve
that she still lives.*
4. Lit.—*This vile woman, what scheme &c.*
5. Lit.—*And what is there in the midst common to Phœbus and
to thee?*
6. Lit.—*To the god to keep.*

Cr.   Well, thou wast then: but now I am *his*, and thou art so no longer.

Ion.   If thou art, thou art impious,[1] but I was pious then.

Cr.   And I slew[2] thee, because thou wast an enemy to my house.

1290   Ion.   I never[3] came in arms into thy land.

Cr.   Yes, most certainly; thou wast going to set the house of Erectheus in a blaze.

Ion.   With what torches, or with what flames of fire?

Cr.   Thou was going to dwell in my home, and take it away in spite of me.

Ion.   'Twas because my father offered me the *rule of* the land which he had won.

1295   Cr.   But how had the descendants of Æolus any share in the land of Pallas?

Ion.   He delivered it by arms, not words.

Cr.   An ally cannot be an original possessor of the soil.

Ion.   And so thou didst attempt to slay me from fear of what?[4]

Cr.   In order that I might not die, *the sure alternative*, if thou shouldst not.

1300   Ion.   Art thou envious, because thou art childless, at my father's having discovered me?

Cr.   Wilt thou then make havoc of the homes of the childless?

Ion.   Nay, but was I to have no share at least of my father's possessions?[5]

---

1. Lit.—*Not pious at least.*
2. If the expression *slew* in the English seems violent, it must be remembered that the aorist in the original is violent also.
3. Force of the negative aorist.
4. Lit.—*From a fear of what, that it should come to pass?*
5. Lit.—*Was there no portion to me (not of thine) but of my father's (property)?*

CR. No more than[1] spear and shield: this is thy whole inheritance.

ION. Quit the altar and the divine abode.

CR. Keep thy exhortations for thy mother, 1305 wherever she is.[2]

ION. And shalt thou attempt to kill me, and not undergo the penalty *of thy crime?*

CR. Yes, if thou art willing to slay me in this sanctuary.

ION. What pleasure is it to thee to die grasping the wreaths[3] of the god?

CR. I shall cause grief to one of those by whom grief has been caused to me.[4]

ION. Alas! 'Tis strange, how unfairly and 1310 without wise counsel the god has laid down his laws to mortals: for the wicked should not have been allowed to take refuge at[5] the altar, but *it should have been permitted* to drive them away from it; for it is not good that evil hand should touch the gods:[6] but the righteous[7] *only*, any one that was wronged, should have been allowed to take refuge in holy 1315 places, and not the man that is good, and the man that is not, to meet together there and have equal *protection* from the gods.

---

1. Lit.—*As much as (and no more)*.
2. Lit.—*Exhort thy mother, wherever she is for thee*. Σοί is the ethical dative, here used with an ironical force. The allusion to Ion's mother is generally considered to involve a "double entente." The hyperbaton of μητέρα is, as Mr. Paley observes, remarkable.
3. This is probably the meaning of ἐν στέμμασι, the ἐν of circumstance.
4. These words are no doubt intended to be ambiguous. *The one* she inwardly meant was *Apollo:* Ion, would understand it of *himself*.
5. Lit.—*To occupy*.
6. Paley follows Hermann's punctuation, which is extremely awkward. There surely should be a colon at χεῖρα.
7. This dative ἐνδίκοις with ἐχρῆν is puzzling.

PYTHIA. Hold, my son: for I have left the divining tripod within[1] this enclosure, and am passing over it with my feet *to come to thee, I,* the prophetess 1320 of Phœbus, chosen out of all the Delphian women according to the ancient custom of the tripod.[2]

ION. Hail, mother dear to me, although thou barest me not.

PY. But at least I was called *thy mother;* and the name is not unpleasing to me.

ION. Hast thou heard how this woman endeavoured to kill me by a plot?

1325 PY. I have heard: and yet thou art doing wrong to be *so* wrathful.

ION. Is it not right that I should in turn destroy those who seek to slay me?

PY. Wives were ever yet hostile to children born before *their marriage.*

ION. Yes, and so are we to step-mothers, if we are ill treated.

PY. *Say* not so. Leave the temple, and going to thy country—

1330 ION. What, I pray, wouldst thou exhort me to do?[3]

PY. With hands pure[4] *from blood-guiltiness* proceed to Athens *attended* by good omens.

ION. Surely *the hands of* every one *are* pure who slays his enemies.

PY. *This do* not thou: but hear from me the words which I have *to tell thee.*

---

1. Lit.—*Of.* See Hermann's or Paley's note on this passage.
2. Lit.—*Preserving the ancient &c.* The two clauses form a sort of hendiadys.
3. Lit.—*Is it right that, being exhorted, I should do?*
4. Lit.—*Purely.*

Ion. Speak: for thou wilt say whatever thou mayest say, in a friendly spirit.[1]

Py. Seest thou this vessel which I am carrying 1335 in my hands?[2]

Ion. I see an old basket decked with chaplets.[3]

Py. In this I found thee once upon a time, a new-born babe.

Ion. What sayest thou? New *to me is* the story *that* has been related.[4]

Py. Yes, for I kept it[5] secret, but now I make it known to thee.

Ion. How hast thou then concealed it from me 1340 so long,[6] if thou didst find me then?

Py. The God wished to keep thee as a minister in his temple.

Ion. And does he not desire *to do so* now? In what way am I to be assured of this?

Py. Having revealed thy father, he bids thee depart from this land.

Ion. And hast thou preserved this by command, or from what motive?

Py. Loxias at the time suggested to my 1345 mind—

Ion. To do what? Say, finish thy story.

Py. To preserve this that I had found, to the present time.

---

1. Lit.—*Being of friendly spirit.*
2. Lit.—*Under-arm load* (probably) *of my hand.* Anything can be put under the *arm* and yet carried with the *hand,* so that the expression seems not so forced as it has been called.
3. Lit.—*In chaplets.* For this ἐν, see note on 1308.
4. Lit.—*Has been brought in.*
5. Lit.—*Those things.*
6. Lit.—*Wast thou concealing it...long since.*

Ion. But what good, or what harm does it do to me ?[1]

Py. Herein are laid up the swaddling-clothes in which thou wast.

1350   Ion. Thou bringest these things forth as helps to discover[2] my mother.

Py. Yes, as the god *so* wills, but did not before.

Ion. O this day of happy omens to me !

Py. Take them therefore, and find her that bore thee. And when thou hast visited all Asia and the limits of Europe, thou wilt learn *about* these 1355 matters thyself. For the sake of the god I reared thee, my son, and I *now* restore to thee these things, which he willed that I should find and keep, though without *express* command : but wherefore he *so* willed, I am not able to say. But none of mortal 1360 beings knew that I had these, nor where they were hidden. And *now* farewell: for I embrace thee *with* equal *affection* as though I had given thee birth. But begin where thou oughtest *to begin* searching for thy mother; first, *enquiring* if any Delphian maid[3] having born thee, *brought thee* to this temple 1365 *and* exposed thee, and next, if any Greek woman.[4] And *now* thou hast learned all from me and from Phœbus, who took part in thy fortunes.

Ion. Alas ! alas ! How I shed the moist tear from my eyes, when I turn my thoughts to the time[5] when she who bore me after furtive embraces, 1370 secretly put me away, and gave me not the breast;

---

1. Lit.—*Does it involve for me ?*
2. Lit.—*Investigations.*
3. Lit.—*Maid of Delphian women.*
4. i. e. *From any other part of Greece.* Ἑλλάς here = Ἑλληνίς, very uncommon.
5. Lit.—*Thither.*

but I passed the life of a servant in the abode of the
god, without a name. The god was good, but
my fate was hard:[1] for at the time that I ought to
have been delicately nurtured[2] in the arms of
my mother, and to have had some enjoyment of life,
I was deprived of my dearest mother's nourishment. 1375
And wretched also is she who bore me, since
she has shared the same fate[3] in losing the joy
of *possessing* a son. And now I will take this
basket and present it an offering to the god, that
I may discover nothing that I would not.[4] For if a
slave happens to have given me birth, to discover my 1380
mother is a worse thing *for me* than to say nought
about her.[5] O Phœbus, I present this to thy temple.
Yet what am I doing? I am opposing the good will
of the god towards me, who has preserved these
tokens of my mother for me. I must open this, 1385
and take heart. For never can I escape from[6]
what is fated. O sacred chaplets,[7] why, I pray, have
ye been hidden from me, and ye bands,[8] by which my
treasures were guarded? Behold the covering of
the round basket, how it has been saved from growing 1390
old by some divine *care*, and the wicker-work is free
from mouldiness:[9] but the interval of time is long
indeed for these hoarded relics *to have lasted.*

---

1. Lit.—*The matters of the god were good, but of fate heavy.*
2. Lit.—*To have lived delicately.*
3. Lit.—*Has experienced the same experience.*
4. Lit.—*Nothing of the things which I do not wish.* The meaning
is—*that none of my discoveries may be of an unhappy nature.*
5. Lit.—*Being silent, to let her be.*
6. Ὑπερβαίην, pass over, leap over, a metaphor from an animal
leaping over a hunting net to escape.
7. See 1336.
8. The fastenings of the ἀντίπηξ.
9. Lit.—*Mould is absent from the things entwined.*

CR. What apparition do I behold of things not *even* hoped for?

Ion. Silence: thou wast an enemy to me before.

1395   CR. I cannot be silent:[1] exhort me not. For I see the basket in which[2] I formerly exposed thee, my child, when thou wast yet a helpless[3] babe, *taking thee to the grotto of Cecrops* and the cavernous Macræ.[4] But I will leave this altar, even if I must die.

400   Ion. Seize this woman; for inspired with a sudden frenzy by the god, she has leaped up and left the sculptured altar;[5] and bind her arms.

CR. Go on to slay me, if ye will;[6] since I will cling both to this and to thee and to what is shut up within *it*.

Ion. Is not this abominable? I am being dragged away on a pretended claim of relationship.[7]

1405   CR. Not so, but thou *near and* dear *to me* art found by one *near and* dear to thee.

Ion. I *near and* dear to thee? And that is the reason why thou wouldst have secretly murdered me?

CR. Yes, thou art my son, if that[8] is *nearest and* dearest to one who bore[9] thee.

Ion. Leave off inventing *falsehoods:* right surely will I take thee.[10]

---

1. Lit.—*My affairs are not in silence.*
2. Lit.—*Where.*
3. Lit.—*Infant, dumb.*
4. This line is suspected, and probably with good reason, as *the grotto of Cecrops* or rather *of Aglauros Cecrops' daughter* was not the same as the *Paneum,* hitherto described as the scene of Creusa's amour.
5. Lit.—*Sculptures of the altar.*
6. Lit.—*Ye would not cease slaying me,* (*if ye did as I bid you*).
7. Lit.—*By reason of mere words.* On ῥυσιάζομαι, comp. 523.
8. Lit.—*This.*
9. Si mulier, de se loquens, pluralem adhibet numerum, genus etiam adhibet masculinum; si masculinum adhibet genus, numerum etiam adhibet pluralem. Dawes' Canon.
10. Ion means—*I will convict thee right well.* She affects to misunderstand him, and answers as though he meant—*I will accept thee as my mother.*

CR. May I arrive at this *happiness;* this, my
son, *is what* I am aiming at.

ION. Is this basket empty, or hides it any 1410
contents?

CR. Yes, thy garments, in which I formerly
exposed thee.

ION. And wilt thou tell the name of them,
before thou seest them?

CR. Yes, and if I tell thee not, I will be bound[1]
to die.

ION. Speak; since thy boldness has *about it*
something passing strange.

CR. Look for the work which I wove when I was 1415
a girl in days gone by.

ION. What sort of work? Many are the works
woven by maidens.

CR. Not a perfect *piece of work*, but such
as a first attempt at the loom *might be.*

ION. What pattern has it? thou must not try to
catch me in this way.[2]

CR. A Gorgon in the central tissue of the robe.

ION. O Jupiter, what destiny *is this that* pursues 1420
me to the end?[3]

CR. And it is bordered with snakes after the
manner of the ægis.

ION. See here! this is the piece of work: *sure*
as an oracle we find it.[4]

CR. O work[5] of my maidenhood found at last.

---

1. Lit.—*I put myself under (an engagement).*
2. Lit.—*That thou mayst not catch me in this way.*
3. 'Εκ, —*to the end.*
4. I have ventured to give a new sense to the words, reading
them θέσφαθ' ὡς εὑρίσκομεν.
5. The accusative (ἱστόν) after ὦ is rare in Greek, though
common after o in Latin.

Ion. Is there anything besides this? or art thou lucky in *guessing at* this alone?

1425   Cr. An antique thing, some snakes with jaws all gold.[1]

Ion. The gift of Minerva, who bids Athenians deck their children with these ornaments?[2]

Cr. Yes, in imitation[3] of *what she did to* Erichthonius of olden time.

Ion. Do what, make what use, tell me, of the golden ornament?

Cr. As a necklace, for a new-born child to wear, my son.

1430   Ion. Here are *the snakes*[4] inside. But I want to know *what* the third thing *is*.

Cr. I put round *thy head* at the time a chaplet of the olive, which Minerva first planted on[5] the rock: which, if it *still* exists, never leaves its greenness, but flourishes as being produced from the original olive.

1435   Ion. O mother most dear to me, with gladness beholding thee I kiss[6] thy glad cheeks.

Cr. O my son, O thou light *of joy* more precious to thy mother than *the light of* the sun (for the god will pardon *this word*), I·hold thee in my arms,[7] a discovery beyond my hopes, who I thought was

---

1. The reading in the text ought to give this sense, but gives none. Toup and Hermann read πάγχρυσοι γένυν, which is good enough. After all, is not the true reading likely to be—δράκοντες ἀρχαῖόν τι πάγχρυσοί γ' ἔνι—*Yes, an antique thing is in it, some snakes all of gold—*? The hyperbaton involves no difficulty.
2. Lit. *Who bids rear children in it.* See 24 seqq.
3. Lit.—*Imitations.*
4. The want of inflection in the English pronoun makes it necessary to repeat the substantive. In Greek the οἵδε is sufficient as necessarily referring to δράκοντες.
5. Lit.—*Introduced to.*
6. Lit.—*I have flung myself upon.*
7. Lit.—*Hands.*

dwelling beneath the earth in the depth with the 1440
shades and Proserpine.

Ion. But, O my dear mother, in thy arms I
seem as he that is dead and *yet* is not dead.

Cr. O thou expanse of the bright sky, what
words shall I utter, shall I cry aloud?[1] Whence
comes it that this unlooked-for delight has happened 1445
to me? Whence *comes it that* I have gotten this joy?

Ion. To me it would at one time have seemed
likely that anything in the world[2] would happen
sooner than this,—that I am thy son.

Cr. I still tremble with fear.

Ion. That thou hast me not, now that thou hast 1450
me?

Cr. *So it seems,* for far away my hopes had I
cast. O lady,[3] from whom, from whom didst thou
receive my babe into thy arms? By what hand came
he to the house of Loxias?

Ion. This was *the work* of the god: but as to the 1455
remainder of our destinies may we be as fortunate
as the former part of them was unfortunate.

Cr. Not without tears wast thou born,[4] my child,
and with sighs wast thou parted from thy mother's
arms: but now, against thy cheek, I *freely* breathe,
having found a joy most blissful.   1460

Ion. What thou sayest is true of thee and me
alike.[5]

Cr. I am no longer childless nor without
offspring: our house is established, and the land has

---

1. Βοάσω—Not future, which would be βοάσομαι, but (as Paley
observes) deliberative subjunctive.
2. Lit.—*It would have presented itself that all things.*
3. The Pythia.
4. Ἐκλοχεύει—Histor. pres.
5. Lit.—*Thou speakest of my matter and thine jointly.*

a prince : and Erechtheus flourishes again in youthful
1465 vigour, and the earth-born race no more looks on
darkness, but is again enlightened by the rays of the
sun.[1]

Ion. My mother, let my father, I pray,[2] come
and share the gladness which I have caused thee.

Cr. My child, my child, what *is't* thou sayest?
How, how am I put to shame.

1470   Ion. How saidst thou?

Cr. Thou wast born to another,[3] to another.

Ion. Ah me! thy maidenhood brought me forth
a spurious son?

Cr. Not *celebrated* by torches nor by dances did
my union, bring thee[4] forth, my son.

1475   Ion. Alas! I was begotten, my mother, of some
ignoble father.[5]

Cr. Bear witness the slayer of the Gorgon—

Ion. What is that[6] thou saidst?

Cr. Who amid[7] my *native* rocks dwells on the
olive-planted hill.

1480   Ion. This that thou tellest me, this is an attempt
to deceive me and no truth.[8]

Cr. At the rock haunted by nightingales with
Phœbus—

Ion. What sayest thou of Phœbus?

---

1. Lit.—*Recovers sight by the torches of the sun.* The metaphor
is expressive of joy and gladness, a sense which the word φῶς
sometimes actually obtains.

2. Mo*i*—the ethical dative.

3. Lit.—*From some other quarter.*

4. Lit.—*Thy head.*

5. Lit.—*Base-born from some quarter.*

6. Lit.—*This.*

7. Lit.—*At.*

8. Lit.—*Crafty and not true.* When words are doubled in Greek,
as λέγεις λέγεις, it will be sometimes necessary, in consequence
partly of the different order of the words, to double some *other* words
in a translation.

CR. Was I united in stealthy love.

Ion. Say *on;* for thou art about to tell me somewhat acceptable and fortunate *to hear.*

CR. And at the tenth revolution of the month, I 1485
brought thee forth, a stealthy child, to Phœbus.

Ion. O thou that hast spoken *words* of greatest
joy, if thou speakest *words* of truth.

CR. And I put on thee to cover thee[1] these
swaddling-clothes the work of thy mother's maidenhood,[2] the clumsy attempts[3] of my shuttle. And 1490
I gave thee not a mother's nurture with milk, nor with
the breast, nor bathings with my hands, but in
solitary cavern, for beaks of birds a prey[4] and feast,
wast thou exposed to die[5] 1495

Ion. O my mother that couldst endure *to commit*
so terrible a deed.

CR. By fear constrained I cast away thy life, **my**
child; 'twas against my will I slew[6] thee

Ion. And thou wast about to die by my hand in 1500
an impious way.

CR. Ah! Ah! terrible was our fate then, and
terrible are these *last* events too: we are tossed to
and fro by misfortunes and back again by good
fortunes, and the gale[7] is *ever* shifting. Be it 1505
constant at *last:* enough are the troubles of the past;
but now there has sprung up a fair wind *to bear us*
forth out of our troubles, my son.

CHO. Let none of men e'er think that aught is
beyond hope, seeing what is happening now.

---

1. Lit.—*Cast about thee.*
2. Lit.—*Maiden swaddling-clothes of thy mother.*
3. Lit.—*Blunders.* See 1417.
4. Lit.—*A slaughter.*
5. Lit.—*For Hades.*
6. On the aorist see Paley's note, and compare 1293.
7. Viz. *Of fortune.*

1510   Ion.   O Fortune that hast in turn caused
        myriads of mortals ere this both to be unfortunate and
        to be prosperous again, to what a point in life's
        career have I arrived in so nearly having killed
        a mother,[1] and in so nearly having suffered an unde-
1515   served *death myself.* Is it possible for the sun's
        bright course to witness[2] all these *freaks of thine* day
        by day? Well then, I have discovered thee, my
        mother, a joyful discovery *for me,* and such an[3] origin,
        in my judgment,[4] is not at all to be despised. But
        the rest I wish to say to thee alone. Come hither;
        for I would whisper[5] my words into thine ear, and
1520   cast the veil of secrecy over the facts.   Be thou sure,
        my mother, that thou didst not first fall into the
        unfortunate error to which maidens are liable with
        regard to secret attachments, and then art laying the
        blame to the god, and art endeavouring to avoid the
1525   disgrace to me by saying that thou borest me to
        Phœbus, when thou borest me by no god at all.[6]

        Cr.   By Minerva the Victorious,[7] who of old
        aided Jove in battle against the giants with her car,
        'tis none of mortals that is father to thee, my son, but
        the same king Loxias that reared thee up.

1530   Ion.   How then *was it that* he gave his son to

---

1. I fear that the exact meaning of this passage has not yet been
thoroughly explained. I have followed Paley.
2. Lit.—*Learn.* This passage again has not been quite satis-
factorily cleared up.
3. Lit.—*This.*
4. 'Ωs ἡμῖν, ἡμῖν being the ethical dative.
5. Lit.—*Speak.*
6. Lit.—*See thou, mother, lest having tripped what irregularities
arise amongst maidens with regard to secret nuptials, thou afterwards
layest the blame to the god, and endeavouring to fly from my dis-
graceful, sayest thou borest me to Phœbus, having borne me not from
a god.* On the indicative after μή, see Paley's note. Νοσήματα is a
cogn. acc. after σφαλεῖσα.
7. Comp. 457, which identifies Νίκη with 'Αθάνα.

another father, and declares that I was born son of Xuthus ?[1]

CR. That thou wast so born, *he says* not, but *though* begotten of him, *to Xuthus* he gives thee: for a friend may give a friend his own son *to be* master of his house.[2]

ION. *Whether* the god is true, or divines falsely, *is a question*, my mother, *which* not without reason disturbs my mind. 1535

CR. Hear now therefore the thoughts which have occurred to me, my son. It is to benefit thee, that[3] Loxias settles thee in a noble family: but, if thou hadst been called the god's, thou wouldst never have had a home entitling thee to full rights of citizen- 1540 ship,[4] nor the name of *any* father. For how *couldst thou*, when I myself wished to conceal my loves, and was for secretly killing thee[5]? And it is to serve thee that[3] he assigns thee to another father.

ION. I am following them up by no means inattentively :[6] but I will go into the temple and enquire 1545 of Phœbus whether I am *the son* of a mortal sire or of Loxias. Ha! Who of the gods appears from the house fragrant with incense and shows a countenance bright with the rays of the sun ?[7] Let us fly,

---

1. Lit.—*That I have been produced from Xuthus a son.*
2. i.e. *His heir.*
3. Lit.—*Benefiting thee. Serving thee.*
4. Lit.—*Of whole inheritance.*
5. Paley's notes on this passage are well worth reading, though no explanation I have seen is quite satisfactory. Οὗ appears to me to be the adverb rather than the pronoun—*where = in a case in which, when.*
6. Lit.—*I am coming after them* (i.e. *thy thoughts, as expressed by thee*) *not so inattentively.* On this meaning of φαύλως, see Paley's note.
7. Lit.—*Who of the gods, coming into view from the house receiving incense, shows a countenance opposite the sun?* The transverse rays of the rising sun (the Attic stage facing N.N.W.) imparted brightness to the countenance of the statues or persons of the gods, as seen by the audience in the theatre. Paley.

1550 my mother, lest we should look upon the gods, if it
is not meet[1] that we should look upon them at the
present time.[1]

  MINERVA. Fly not: for *I am* not an enemy *that*
·ye *should* fly from me, but friendly to you both
in Athens and here. For *it is* I, Pallas, *that* am
come, *the deity* giving a name to thy land, having in
1555 haste sped hither from Apollo, who thought not fit to
present himself to you,[2] lest reproaches for the past
should interrupt,[3] but he sends me to speak to you the
message that this lady bore thee by Apollo
for thy father, and he gives thee to whom he gave
thee, not as having begotten thee, but that he
1560 (Xuthus) may take thee into a family of most noble
birth. And when this purpose[4] was disclosed and revealed to him (Xuthus), fearing that thou wouldst be
slain by the plots of thy mother, and that she *would be
slain* by thee, he rescued *you both* by plans which he
devised. And king *Apollo* intended still to remain
1565 silent about these things and[5] to make this lady
known *to thee* as thy *mother* in Athens, and *to her*
that thou wast born[6] of her and Phœbus as thy sire.
But, that I may complete the business for the god,
and fully explain[7] his divine will, for the sake of
which I yoked my chariot, listen to me. Creusa, take
1570 this youth and go to the Cecropian land, and seat him
on the royal throne: for he, being born of the line of

---

1. Lit.—*It is not the season.*
2. Lit.—*To come into your sight.*
3. Lit.—*Should intervene.*
4. Lit.—*Thing.* The *purpose* was of course *the intention to give
him to Xuthus for a son.*
5. Lit.—*Having throughout been silent about them.*
6. Lit.—*Thee, that thou wast born.*
7. Περαίνω, the verb common to the two members of the sentence,
hardly admits of one translation suitable to both objects.

Erechtheus, has a right to rule my land. And he shall
be famous throughout Hellas: for his sons, four born
from one root, shall give their names to the land, and 1575
to the people of the country arranged by tribes who
inhabit my rock. Teleon shall be the first: then
next the Hopletes, and the Argades, and the
Ægicores, *named* from my Ægis, shall possess one
tribe *each*.[1] And the sons born in turn to them in 1580
course of time decreed shall occupy the island towns
of the Cyclades, and the continent along the coast,[2]
which will give[3] strength to my country; and they
shall inhabit the plains of two continents, the land of
Asia and of Europe, on opposite sides of the strait:[4] 1585
and named Ionians for the name's sake of this *youth*,
they shall have renown. But to Xuthus and thee
shall be born[5] a common offspring, Dorus, from whom[6]
the Dorian state shall *arise, and* be celebrated in
song; and the second, Achæus, in the land of Pelops,[7]
who shall be lord of the sea-coast near Rhium, and 1590
the people shall be distinguished by being called after
his name.[8] And well has Apollo brought all to pass.
In the first place, he makes thy delivery free from
sickness, so that thy friends knew it not: and when

---

1. Pallas' meaning seems to be, that the four original tribes of
Attica should get their names, Teleontes, Hopletes, Ergades, Ægicores,
from Ion's four sons, Teleon, Hoples, Argades and Ægicoreus (αἰγίς,
κόρη). See Paley's note.
2. Alluding to the Ionian colonies in Asia Minor.
3. Lit.—*Gives.*
4. Viz. *The Hellespont.*
5. Lit.—*Is born.*
6. Lit.—*Whence.*
7. *The Peloponnesus.*
8. If the reading of this line is correct, it is by no means easy to see
the construction of the words. The least objectionable way of taking
them appears to me λαὸς ἐπισημανθήσεται (ὥστε) ἐπώνυμος κεκλῆσθαι
ὄνομα κείνου.

1595 thou barest[1] this thy son, and hadst exposed him[2] in swaddling-clothes, he requests Mercury to snatch up the babe in his arms and convey him hither, and he reared him and suffered him not to die.[3] Now therefore keep it secret that this youth is thy son, that

1600 Xuthus may be pleased with the belief that he is his,[4] and that thou, lady, on thy part mayst enjoy thy own blessings.[5] And *now* fare ye well: for, after this rest from your troubles, I announce to you a happy destiny.

ION. O Pallas daughter of Jove supreme, I will

1605 accept thy words with no want of faith: for I believe that I am born of Loxias *for* my father and of this lady: and even before this was not incredible *to me*.

CR. Hear me then. I praise Phœbus though I praised him not before, because he restores to me the son whom he once neglected. And of pleasant aspect to me are these gates and *this* oracle of the

1610 god, though before they were hateful. And now I am pleased to linger with my hand upon the knocker and to seek admission at the gates.[6]

MIN. I commend[7] thee, because thou art changed and praisest the god: the *aid* of the gods was ever wont to be long in coming, 'tis true,[8] but at last 'tis mighty.[9]

CR. My son, let us go home.

MIN. Go ye, and I will bring you on your way.

---

1. Lit.—*Proceededst to bear*—imperf.
2. Κάτέθου = not καὶ ἐπέθου, but καὶ ἀπέθου.
3. Lit.—*Breathe out his life.*
4. Lit.—*That his belief may pleasingly possess Xuthus.*
5. Lit.—*Mayst go having the good things of thyself.*
6. Lit.—*We gladly hang as to hands from the knocker and speak to the gates.*
7. Lit.—See note on 1269.
8. Lit.—*Somehow.*
9. Lit.—*Not weak.*

Ion.   A noble escort have we.[1]   1615
Cr.   Yes, and one that loves the city.
Min.   And take thy place on the ancient throne.
Ion.   A noble possession is it for me.[2]
Cho.   Farewell, Apollo, son of Jove and Latona.
He whose house is vexed with calamities, must
reverence the gods and be of good courage : for at
last the good obtain their due, but the wicked shall 1620
never prosper—such as their nature is, such is their
lot.[3]

---

1. Lit.—*The guardian of our way is a worthy one at least.*
2. Lit.—*The possession is a worthy one for me.*
3. Paley explains the last few words extremely well—ὥσπερ
κακοί εἰσι τὴν φύσιν, οὕτω καὶ κακῶς ἀεὶ πράξουσι.

Cambridge:
Printed by J. Hall & Son.

J. Hall and Son's
LIST OF PUBLICATIONS.

———◆———

By the Rev. Dr. PINNOCK,

Scripture History ;
An Analysis of, (*Dedicated, by permission, to the Lord Bishop of Llandaff.*) Intended for Readers of OLD TESTAMENT HISTORY; with a *Copious Index and Examination Questions*, Twelfth Edition. 18mo cloth 3*s.* 6*d.*

New Testament History ;
An Analysis of, (*Dedicated, by permission, to the Regius Professor of Divinity.*) Embracing the Criticism and Interpretation of the original Text; *with Questions for Examination.* Ninth Edition. 18mo cloth 4*s.*

Ecclesiastical History ;
An Analysis of, (*Dedicated, by permission, to the late Norrisian Professor of Divinity.*) From the Birth of Christ, to the Council of Nice, A. D. 325. *With Examination Questions, A New Edition, greatly Improved.* 18mo cloth 3*s.* 6*d.*

The History of the Reformation ;
Analysis of, (*Dedicated, by permission, to the Lord Bishop of Ely*) with the prior and subsequent History of the English Church ; *and Examination Questions.* Fifth Edition. 18mo cloth 4*s.* 6*d.*

A Short Analysis of Old Testament History, or Scripture Facts ; With *numerous*
Questions. Fourth Edition. 18mo cloth, 1*s.* 6*d.*

Rubrics for Communicants ;
Explanatory of the HOLY COMMUNION OFFICE, with Prayers, Aids to Examination, and Scripture Illustrations, (to be used in Churches). 18mo cloth, 1*s.* 6*d.*

LAWS and USAGES of the Church and the Clergy ;

The Curate and Unbeneficed Clerk	Vol. A.	5/6
The Officiating Minister	Vol. B.	5/6
The Ornaments of the Church	Vol. C.	5/6
The Ornaments of the Minister	Vol. D.	5/6
The Order and Ritual of Public Worship	Vol. E.	5/6
Morning Prayer, Evening Prayer, Litany, and The Holy Communion (the concluding Volume)	Vol. F.	6/6

Each Volume complete in its own subject, and may be had *separately* :—

*** VOL. C. "*The Ornaments of the Church*" is now being reprinted with considerable alterations, and will be ready shortly

----

Wake's Apostolical Epistles ;

Being the genuine EPISTLES of the APOSTOLICAL FATHERS, translated by WILLIAM WAKE, D.D., late Archbishop of Canterbury. *New Edition*, carefully revised. Cr. 8vo. 5s.

Paley's Evidences of Christianity ;

Comprising the Text of Paley, verbatim; *Examination Questions* at the foot of each page, and a full Analysis prefixed to each Chapter. By Rev. GEORGE FISK, LL.B. Prebendary of Lichfield. *Fourth Edition.* Cr. 8vo cloth, 4s. 6d.

Compendium Theologicum, or Manual for

STUDENTS in Theology, by the Rev. O. ADOLPHUS. *Third Edition.* Considerably Enlarged. cr. 8vo. *cloth*, 6s. 6d.

The Creed and the Church ; a Hand-Book

of THEOLOGY; being a SYNOPSIS of Pearson on the Creed; and of Hooker's Ecclesiastical Polity, Book V., with brief Papers on Heresies and Schisms; Life and Epistles of St Paul; History of the Book of Common Prayer; XXXIX Articles, &c., by REV. EDGAR SANDERSON, B.A., late Scholar of Clare College. Post 8vo. cloth, 3s

---

BY THE REV. W. TROLLOPE, M.A.

Liturgy and Ritual ;

A Practical and Historical Commentary on, With copious *Examination Questions*, Cr. 8vo cloth, 5s

"To enable Divinity Students and Candidates for Holy Orders to master this important branch of Theological Learning the above is admirably adapted............We hope it will be brought into extensive use."— *Literary Churchman.*

(*The above is much used for the Theological Examinations at Cambridge.*)

The Acts of the Apostles ;

A Commentary on, *with Examination Questions*, chiefly selected from University Examination Papers; especially intended for Candidates preparing for the B. A. Degree. *Fourth Edition*, with considerable improvements. Cr. 8vo cloth, 4s.

The Gospel of St Matthew ;

Questions and Answers on. *Second Edition*, 12mo cloth, 4s.

The Gospel of St Luke ;

A Commentary on, *with Examination Questions*, accompanied by References to the Text at the foot of each page. *Second Edition.* 12mo cloth, 4s.

XXXIX Articles of the Church of England ;

Questions and Answers on the, *Improved and enlarged. Fifth Edition*, 18mo cloth 2s. 6d.

Liturgy of the Church of England ;

Questions and Answers on the. *Sixth Edition.* 18mo cloth 2s.

J. Hall & Son's List of Publications.

By the Rev. W. GORLE, M.A.

Rector of Whatcote, Warwickshire.

Butler's Analogy, a New Analysis of,
With *Questions*. Second Edition. 18mo cloth, 3s.

Pearson on the Creed;
An Analysis of, with *Examination Questions*. Third Edition. 18mo cloth, 4s.

Hooker, Book V., an Analysis of,
With *Examination Questions*. Second Edition. 18mo cloth, 4s.]

Paley's Horæ Paulinæ;
An Analysis of, *with Examination Questions*.

In the Press.

EURIPIDES, — separate PLAYS of,
Literally Translated, with Notes :—

> ALCESTIS, 12mo, *sewed*, 1/-
> ANDROMACHE, 12mo. *sewed*, 1/-
> BACCHÆ, 12mo. *sewed*, 1/-
> HECUBA, 12mo. *sewed*, 1/-
> HERACLIDÆ, 12mo. *sewed*, 1/-
> HIPPOLYTUS, 12mo. *sewed*, 1/-
> MEDEA, 12mo. *sewed*, 1/-
> ORESTES, 12mo. *sewed*, 1/-
> PHŒNISSÆ, 12mo. *sewed*, 1/-

SOPHOCLES, the Tragedies;
A *Literal Translation* of. Second Edition. 12mo bds 5s.;

Or Translations of the following Plays, separately :—

> AJAX, 12mo. *sewed*, 1/-
> ANTIGONE, 12mo. *sewed*, 1/-
> ELECTRA, 12mo. *sewed*, 1/-
> ŒDIPUS COLONEUS, 12mo. *sewed*, 1/-
> ŒDIPUS the KING, 12mo. *sewed*, 1/-
> PHILOCTETES, 12mo. *sewed*, 1/-
> TRACHINIÆ, 12mo. *sewed*, 1/-

Xenophon's Anabasis, Books III. & IV.,
From the Text of Bornemann and Dindorf, with English Notes. and a LITERAL TRANSLATION. By the Rev. EDGAR SANDERSON, B.A., late Scholar of Clare College. Cr. 8vo interleaved, 5/-

An Easy Practical Hebrew Grammar;

With Exercises for translation from Hebrew into English, and from English into Hebrew: with a KEY to the EXERCISES. By the Rev. P. H. MASON, M. A. Fellow and Hebrew Lecturer of St John's Coll., Cambridge; and the late Dr. H. H. BERNARD. 2 vols. 8vo. cloth, 28s.

The ELEMENTARY PART may be had separately, 8vo. *sewed*, 2s.

Progressive Exercises on the Composition of Greek Prose;

By the Rev. B. W. BEATSON, M.A. Fellow of Pembroke College. *Third Edition, enlarged,* 12mo. cloth limp, 2s.

Cicero Pro Milone;

Translated into Literal English. By a Graduate. 12mo. *sewed*, 2s.

Demosthenes Contra Midiam,

A *Literal Translation* of, by G. BURGESS, M. A. *Second Edition.* 12mo. *sewed*, 2s.

Demosthenes' Three Olynthiac Orations,

A *Literal Translation* of, 12mo *sewed*, 1s.

Demosthenes, First Philippic and Oration

" DE PACE," a *Literal Translation* of, with Notes, 12mo. *sewed*, 1s.

Herodotus, Book III.,

With *English Notes,* and a *Literal Translation,* 12mo interleaved, 3/6 The GREEK separately with English Notes, 2s. 6d.

Herodotus, Book VIII.,

With *English Notes,* by P. J. F. GANTILLON, M. A. 12mo. 2s. 6d

Homer's Iliad, Books III. & IV.,

With *English Notes.* Cr. 8vo 2s. 6d.

Homer's Iliad, XX, XXI, XXII.,

With *English Notes.* Cr. 8vo 2s. 6d.

Persæ of Æschylus,

A *Literal Translation* of, 12mo *sewed*, 1s.

Virgilii Æneidos, Lib. V. and VI.

With Notes, chiefly Grammatical and Explanatory, and an accurate *English Translation.* By E. T. CROOKE, B.A., late of Pembroke College, Cambridge. Cr. 8vo. Interleaved, 5s.

J. Hall & Son, Printers, Cambridge.